loomsbury Farm

nolensville, TN   est. 2009

nnically grown fruits, veggies i herb

Spring Meadow Farm

CHRISTIANA, TN

RIDE Champion 10¢

If It Makes You Healthy

If It Makes You Healthy

More Than 100 Delicious Recipes Inspired by the Seasons

SHERYL CROW and **CHUCK WHITE**

with Mary Goodbody • photographs by Victoria Pearson

ST. MARTIN'S PRESS ❄ NEW YORK

This book is not intended to provide medical advice. Readers, especially those with existing health problems, should consult their physician or health care professional before adopting certain dietary choices.

IF IT MAKES YOU HEALTHY. Copyright © 2011 by Sheryl Crow and Chuck White. All rights reserved. Printed in the United States of America. For information, address St. Martin's Press, 175 Fifth Avenue, New York, N.Y. 10010.

ISBN 978-0-312-65895-3

Photographs by Victoria Pearson,
except for the following: page 2, courtesy of Sheryl Crow;
pages 8–9, 12, and 13 copyright Chris Hudson Photography.

Book Design by Susan Walsh

Production Manager: Adriana Coada

Food Stylist: Valerie Aikman-Smith

Prop Stylist: Pam Morris

Photo Assistant: Jon Nakano

First Edition: April 2011

10   9   8   7   6   5   4   3   2   1

For my mother, Bernice, who is my hero and my favorite chef.

—SHERYL

*For all the amazing people in my life. Most importantly, I would
be nothing without God...anything is possible with Him.*

—CHUCK

Contents

Foreword

November 1, 2010

I met Sheryl Crow in her kitchen, of all places, in 2006. It was an inviting and comfortable room with well-used pots and an overflowing pantry; just a perfect space to discuss nutrition. You would have never guessed that she had just been diagnosed with breast cancer and was currently undergoing radiation therapy. She was dressed simply in faded jeans and a white T-shirt with her beautiful hair effortlessly pulled back. And though she beamed her famous and carefree smile, her eyes said that she was downright determined to learn everything she could from me. She was like a kid on the first day of school.

She jumped feetfirst and with good humor into the sustainable nutritional action plan I devised for her, which emphasized a serious dose of fiber, essential fatty acids, and other cancer-fighting foods. When it comes to nutrition, Sheryl clearly grasps that *she* is in the driver's seat and it is up to her to maximize her knowledge about optimal wellness and eating in the most preventative and life-affirming way. In following such a nutritional agenda, tastiness and ease are the keys to success. While clinical research has shown that we cannot ignore the role of nutrition in preventative health, nothing says we have to sacrifice pleasure at the table.

One of the first things Sheryl did in the weeks after our meeting was hire Chuck White, who cooks like an Iron Chef and yet is as sweet as a spring morning in his native state of Tennessee. He has been cooking for her and her crew ever since—often going on the road to make sure Sheryl eats right while she is on tour. Chuck somehow always manages to find fresh ingredients wherever Sheryl's schedule takes them, preparing meals that burst with appealing, nutrient-rich dishes. (The first time I met Chuck he prepared a dish I can only describe as omega-madness: A pecan-crusted trout served with quinoa noodles, which were to die for.) Believe me: Everyone wants to eat at Sheryl's table before a concert.

And everyone wants to eat at Sheryl's table at home, too: Sheryl's boys, Wyatt and Levi, gravitate to the kitchen when either Chuck or Mommy is cooking. Wyatt already eats just about everything his mom does and joins her at the dinner table every night, whether it's on the road or at home. Although Levi is still too young for much of the food that Sheryl eats, he will clearly benefit in the long run from her devotion to eating right. Having kids of my own, I know how gratifying it is to instill the little ones with healthful eating habits at an early age.

It's clear where Sheryl learned this altruism from—*her* own mother. When Sheryl was diagnosed, Bernice flew to Los Angeles. As soon as she arrived, she set about filling the freezer to the brim with batches of homemade nutritious soups she knew would appeal to her daughter. Describing these soups is easy: Think "creative-meets-nutritious…hello delicious!" Aren't moms the best? Clearly, Bernice's take-charge attitude and selfless passion run deep in the Crow family.

What I love most about *If It Makes You Healthy* is its realistic approach to cooking. Chuck incorporates the concept that it's okay to be a little indulgent every once in a while. He and Sheryl both believe that what matters is how you eat *most of the time*—and that *some of the time* it's okay to take a few liberties. His meals all start with antioxidant-bursting vegetables and from there he keeps things easy and simple. When special occasions arise, he adds a little opulence to the meal but never goes over the top.

Thank you Sheryl and Chuck for assembling a delicious collection of recipes supported by accessible information. *If It Makes You Healthy* is sure to reward anyone who reads it. Leave it to the rock star and her ingenious chef to show the rest of us how to do it right!

—RACHEL S. BELLER, MS, RD
Founder, Beller Nutritional Institute, LLC

Introduction

When I was a kid growing up in Kennett, Missouri, life was pretty simple. I could walk to school every day, I could ride my bike anywhere in town, and I could always count on six o'clock dinner.

Dinnertime in the Crow household was a nightly event. Every evening, my family sat down to a tasty, well-balanced meal lovingly prepared by my mother. Mealtime was a wonderful ritual comprised of discussing the day's events at school and any other topics that might come up—no matter how busy our schedules would ultimately become, dinner was rarely missed.

My mother was and continues to be an excellent cook. She has always been someone who finds enjoyment in reading recipes. Considering there was no authentic ethnic food and certainly nothing consciously raised organic in my southern Missouri town, my mom always tried to be creative—I think she was the first person in our neighborhood to own a wok

(although I vividly remember my father saying, "What are *peanuts* doing in the chicken!?). For the most part, we ate very Midwestern fare: pot roast, fried chicken, mashed potatoes, and gravy. And cholesterol was never in short supply.

Because my mom was such a good cook, I never really took any interest in learning how to cook myself. Instead, I was one of four designated table-setters. When I left home, I didn't bother to learn because by then I had only myself to cook for. Meals were grabbed on the go, except on social occasions, and with a busy recording and touring life I found I lived mostly off hotel room service menus, tuna salad sandwiches in the dressing room, and overcooked catering spreads. It wasn't until I was diagnosed with breast cancer in February of 2006 that I began paying close attention to the foods I put into my body.

Eating for Good Health

My cancer diagnosis was a real game changer for me, someone who has always been fit and healthy, although not a healthy eater by any stretch of the imagination. My cancer diagnosis screamed "vulnerable" to me. Never once in my life had I really considered what I put into my body as having a direct connection to my wellness. Aside from the conventional treatment for my breast cancer, my oncologist suggested I meet with a nutritionist. That's when I was introduced to Rachel Beller, an extraordinary nutritionist, and I quickly became an enthusiastic student of wellness and nutrition. It just made sense to me. I learned the benefits of nutrients such as omega-3 (a fatty acid with disease-fighting properties), and lycopene (found primarily in tomatoes and which has been shown to help prevent cancer), and began to eat what I call an Eskimo diet—lots of salmon, brown rice, and colorful vegetables, the rule being whenever possible to eat the colorful version of a vegetable. I completed radiation in April, two months after the diagnosis, and headed out for a summer tour. Because it's always been challenging to eat healthfully on the road, I decided to hire a chef to cook for the band, the crew, and me. Not only did Chuck White come highly recommended, he really was an answered prayer on my road to eating for a healthy future.

Chuck White Enters My Life

Chuck is modest and laid-back—he reminds me of a surfer—and I immediately fell in love with what he did with food. I wanted Chuck to continue with the nutritional path I was following so I connected him with Rachel. It was clear to both Rachel and me that Chuck had already been mastering cooking for health and wellness and was very current on all the latest dietary studies and information.

Chuck approaches cooking the way I approach songwriting. Just as I've grown up listening to great artists and building a repertoire of influences, he seems to have a dictionary of cooking references. He doesn't reinvent the wheel, but rather notes my particular tastes and pays careful attention to my health concerns and my energy level.

Being on the road so much and not being a great cook at home, I had become stuck in a rut eating the same things over and over, and Chuck has brought diversity and originality to my day. He was already incorporating into his own approach to cooking the steps that the nutritionist had recommended, but he has taken the job a hundred times further. He cooks with foods that are good for me and that I like, and presents them in original and inspiring ways that are always delicious and often surprising. For example, incorporating lycopene into my diet is tricky because I'm not a huge fan of tomatoes, but Chuck came up with delicious soups with simple and unobtrusive tomato bases. I wanted to eat a lot of fish for the omega-3 nutrients that reduce inflammation, but found myself bored with grilled salmon and halibut. Chuck came to the rescue, never being at a loss for ways to prepare fish that were fresh and original.

My nutritionist had suggested eating the more colorful version of any given vegetable whenever possible, because they have the most nutrients. Already being an ardent produce lover, Chuck introduced me to coleslaw made with just-picked purple cabbage that is full of vitamins. He visits both the farmers' market and supermarket and picks out what is freshest or in season. He selects produce with the brightest purples or oranges and whatever is highest in nutrients, and builds

a meal around it. All this for someone who never realized that potatoes and cauliflower came in colors other than white!

Chuck's dishes incorporate spices that have cancer-fighting properties, such as cinnamon and cumin. There is much to know about spices that can be beneficial to general wellness and disease prevention and that each of us can easily incorporate into our daily nutrition routine.

As important as my health is and regardless of how dedicated I am to eating healthfully, I'm also a believer in the 10 percent cheat zone. This explains why I think it's important to have dessert. Chuck manages to make desserts that are tasty and extremely inventive—and still pretty healthy! For example, he makes a chocolate mousse thickened with avocado—which is truly amazing and maybe has to be tasted to be believed (the recipe is on page 238). He also grills juicy summer peaches and fills them with lavender-infused cream cheese (page 117).

Motherhood Changed Me Even More

Since I've become a mother, my appreciation for Chuck has grown even stronger. My kids are the most important part of my life, and like every mom, I want to nourish them with the best, most healthful food possible. I consider myself lucky that I have access to great food and recipes—thanks to Chuck's mentoring—that help their little bodies grow and thrive. I think the real struggle with feeding kids is being creative and not giving in to the mac-and-cheese box or the frozen chicken fingers, but instead finding ways to give them the tastes they love in a healthy way.

It's also important to me that my children grow up eating the same dishes I eat at mealtime. It's the way it was in my house growing up. In fact, I remember my mother saying on numerous occasions when one of us would complain about wanting something other than what we were having for that particular meal, "Do I look like a short-order cook?!" That's why I love dishes such as Chuck's quinoa pasta or his corn chowder, which happens to have popcorn sprinkled on top. What kid doesn't love popcorn? I know Wyatt does; and meanwhile, we are eating healthfully.

I have said time and again that I have been fortunate enough to travel the world and to eat in some of the best and most famous restaurants. I've eaten meals cooked by some of the most recognizable and most successful chefs in the business, but I can honestly say that the best meals I've ever had have been right here in my own home outside Nashville, where I live with Wyatt and Levi. In this book, I want to welcome readers into my kitchen and introduce them to Chef Chuck, the man who changed everything for me. I hope my readers will then set off on their own path toward a better, healthier way of living for them and their families.

A WORD FROM CHUCK

Before you read this book and try the recipes, let me explain how Sheryl and I feel about eating meat, poultry, and fish. We believe all animals deserve to be raised in their natural environments, whether that is deep in the ocean or an open pasture. When I cook for Sheryl and others, I make every effort to find responsibly, humanely raised beef, pork, chicken, and seafood. I look for wild-caught salmon, free-range chicken, grass-fed beef, and heritage pork. I talk to the purveyors at farmers' markets and visit farms near Nashville—or wherever I'm cooking—to uncover the best meat and poultry available.

Throughout the book, I write about these animals and offer tips and advice for finding them for your own table. Take advantage of the growing number of farmers' markets and seek out suppliers that ship high-quality and well-raised meats and chicken. Talk to your fishmonger and find out where he gets his fish and ask for the freshest he has. This is our soapbox. Our shared philosophy is woven through the book and is something about which we care deeply. We don't aim to hit you over the head with it, but we do hope you will come to appreciate how important these products are to our environment and health—and how great they taste.

On the Road

Spring and Summer

It's a real challenge to eat healthfully on the road. Yet there is an emotional relationship to food that can really build the morale of the band, or deflate it. No one wants to eat overcooked food that has been sitting too long on the catering table, and so I depend on Chuck to prepare tasty, nutritious meals for my band and my family and me—nothing too heavy, too sweet, or too spicy, since we have to perform.

Supper on the road is more than grabbing a quick meal. It's a time for fellowship, which, for all of us, is as important as the actual gig. I believe it is a lot to ask people to leave their families and friends and travel across the country for weeks on end to support me, so it's really important to me that they feel loved and appreciated and taken care of. Taking Chef Chuck on the road with me is a gift to all of us. He gives us something to look forward to every time we sit down together to eat, and at the same time his food is giving us the energy and sustenance we need to do our very best when we walk out onstage.

SC DAILY VENUE SHEET 2010

Today is:	Thursday Aug 19
Today we:	Verizon Amphitheater
	Alpharetta, GA

Today's Timings:

Load In:	9:00 AM
SC Sound Check:	4:00 to 5:00 PM
CC Sound Check:	5:30 to 6:00 PM
Dinner:	5:00 PM
Doors:	7:00 PM
CC on Stage:	7:50 PM
Changeover:	8:40 PM to 9:00 PM
SC on stage:	9:00 PM
Curfew:	11:00 PM

After Show:

Bus to Memphis - 8 Hours

Since Wyatt and Levi came along, life on the road is distinctly different from how it used to be. All the drugs, sex, and rock-and-roll . . . well, they never really existed on our tours to begin with, but suffice it to say that any sort of remnant of past rock-and-roll touring has been replaced by books and toys, bottle warmers and diapers, a bike with training wheels and a blow-up swimming pool. The key is to make the bus seem as much like home as possible. It's the same with snacks. Chuck has always done an amazing job of creating snacks and stocking the bus with gluten-free munchies, fruits, and all sorts of yummy fare for a three-year-old. Levi is working on getting some teeth so he can eventually eat what big brother eats!

I love touring. I love interacting with the audience, standing up in front of a full house and sharing my music. I cannot lie—it is an odd way to live. We go to sleep in one town and wake up in another. My kids don't know a different life, with the exception of when we are at home at the farm, and so it's important that they stay healthy and active. This means a balanced and healthful diet, but it also means that I make our time together rich and fun. So, when we're on the road, I make every effort to do something special with Wyatt every day. This might be a visit to a local zoo, children's museum, or water park. I feel extremely lucky that while my boys are both young, I can do my work and not miss out on anything they are doing, especially since I go to work after bath, books, bottle, prayers, and bed.

Appetizers and Snacks

Bruschetta with Tofu Spread
and Summer Vegetables

CHUCK: *Classic bruschetta, made by topping garlic-rubbed toast with sliced tomatoes, basil, and onions, can't be beat in the summer when vegetables and herbs are at their height of ripeness, and this recipe is no exception. The tofu spread bursts with flavors that complement the tomatoes and cukes, while the pickled red onions add their own special hints of sweet and sour. The tofu spread is endlessly versatile, as it can be daubed on other sandwiches or served with crackers as a dip.*

Serves 8

8 ounces extra-firm tofu, pressed, see Try Cooking with Tofu on page 18

2 tablespoons freshly squeezed lemon juice

1 tablespoon finely chopped flat-leaf parsley

1½ teaspoons Dijon mustard

½ teaspoon garlic powder

¼ cup light olive oil (or 2 tablespoons extra-virgin olive oil and 2 tablespoons canola oil)

Kosher salt and freshly ground black pepper

8 slices whole-grain bread, lightly toasted

4 to 5 medium-size ripe tomatoes, preferably organic, cored and sliced

16 slices English cucumber

½ cup Pickled Red Onions, page 221

¼ cup roughly chopped assorted fresh herbs, such as basil, oregano, parsley, and chives

1. Cut the pressed tofu into small chunks and transfer them to the bowl of a food processor fitted with the metal blade. Add the lemon juice, parsley, mustard, and garlic powder and pulse 10 to 15 times. Scrape down the sides of the bowl with a rubber spatula and then pulse for about 15 seconds.

2. With the food processor running, slowly drizzle the oil through the feed tube into the tofu mixture, blending until it is the consistency of mayonnaise, 2 to

3 minutes. If necessary, thin the tofu with water, 1 teaspoon at a time. Season to taste with salt and pepper, and pulse to mix. Set aside until ready to use, or transfer to a container with a tight-fitting lid and refrigerate for up to 10 days.

3. Spread about 1 tablespoon of tofu spread on each slice of toast. Top with the tomato and cucumber slices and season to taste with salt and pepper.

4. Top each open-faced sandwich with pickled onions and a generous sprinkling of fresh herbs.

TRY COOKING WITH TOFU

Also called bean curd, tofu is sold according to texture: silken, soft, medium, firm, and extra-firm. It's ivory colored and mild tasting—and for those who eat it regularly, it's just about a perfect protein.

Tofu nearly always is sold packed in water and before it's cooked, it should be drained, rinsed, and drained again. It usually comes in one-pound blocks and for some recipes should be weighted (pressed) for about an hour. To do so, put the drained tofu on top of several layers of paper towels on a plate, top it with another plate, and set a can or heavy pan that weighs about a pound on top of the plate. Let this construction stand for about an hour, during which time excess moisture will be released.

Roasted Summer Vegetable Panini with Goat Cheese

CHUCK: *A roasted vegetable panini is a welcome light lunch, afternoon snack, or quick preconcert meal. I make them with just about any and all vegetables—Sheryl never complains!—but this mixture of peppers, squash, and mushrooms is one of our favorites. The balsamic vinegar gives the veggies deep-throated sweetness, while the goat cheese provides delicious creaminess and eliminates the need for any sort of mayonnaise or other dressing.* Serves 4

2 portobello mushrooms, stems and gills removed, sliced

1 red bell pepper, seeded, membranes removed, and julienned

1 large yellow squash, cut into ¼-inch-thick slices

1 large zucchini, cut into ¼-inch-thick slices

4 tablespoons extra-virgin olive oil, plus more for brushing on the panini

2 tablespoons balsamic vinegar

2 teaspoons dried thyme

2 teaspoons garlic powder

Kosher salt and freshly ground black pepper

2 wholegrain or whole-wheat French baguettes, about 12 inches long

4 to 6 ounces soft goat cheese

1½ cups fresh spinach

1. Preheat the oven to 400°F. Line a baking sheet with aluminum foil and lightly oil it with olive oil.
2. In a large bowl, toss the mushrooms, bell pepper, yellow squash, and zucchini together. Drizzle the vegetables with the olive oil and vinegar and toss to coat evenly. Add the thyme and garlic powder and season to taste with salt and pepper, tossing to evenly distribute the seasonings.
3. Spread the vegetables on the baking sheet and roast for about 15 minutes or until the vegetables are fork tender and their colors have perked up. There is no need to stir the vegetables as they roast.

4 Meanwhile, slice the baguette in half lengthwise. Spread the goat cheese on the top half of each.

5. Remove the vegetables from the oven and reduce the oven temperature to 350°F.

6. Arrange the roasted vegetables on the bottom half of each baguette and top with spinach. Press the tops of the baguettes on the spinach and cut each sandwich in half for 4 sandwiches.

7. Line the baking sheet with a fresh sheet of foil and put the halved baguettes on the center of the baking sheet. Brush the top of the sandwiches with olive oil and then top with a sheet of foil.

8. Put a second baking sheet over the top of the sandwiches and press down on the sheet to compress the sandwiches. (You can also top the sandwiches with a heavy saucepan or sauté pan to weight them.) Transfer both baking sheets to the oven and bake the panini for 10 to 12 minutes or until the bread is golden and crusty and the goat cheese is oozing from the sides of the sandwiches.

9. Carefully remove the panini from between the baking sheets and put on a cutting board. Cut the halves in half again.

Lime-Kissed Stuffed Avocados

CHUCK: *I make these stuffed avocados pretty regularly when we're on the road. Everyone loves them because just about everyone likes avocados and they are filling without being heavy—the perfect snack or light meal.* Serves 4

4 ripe avocados

4 teaspoons fresh lime juice

1½ teaspoons kosher salt

1 teaspoon ground cumin

1 teaspoon garlic powder

½ teaspoon black pepper

4 tablespoons fresh store-bought salsa, preferably organic

Blue corn or flax seed tortillas, preferably organic

1. Cut the avocados into halves and remove pits. Carefully scoop the flesh from each avocado, leaving the skins intact so that you can refill them. Transfer the avocado flesh to a glass mixing bowl. Add the lime juice, salt, cumin, garlic powder, and pepper and mash with a fork or potato masher. Taste and adjust the seasoning.

2. Spoon the avocado back into the scooped-out skins. Garnish the top of each with a tablespoon of fresh salsa.

3. Serve with organic blue corn or flax seed tortillas.

AVOCADOS, AVOCADOS, AVOCADOS

I repeat the word three times because Sheryl and I just can't get enough. Luckily, they are easy to come by just about anywhere, with the large winter crops coming into the stores in January and February. To tell if an avocado is ripe, hold it in your hand and exert gentle pressure. It should give nicely, but not feel mushy (similar to determining the ripeness of a peach).

You can buy hard avocados and let them ripen on the counter, but that can take up to a week. To speed up the ripening process, place the avocados in a paper bag with an apple or banana, and they should ripen in a day or so. Avocados are packed with good stuff for your body: They may contain more fat than other fruits, but the fat is a "good" one—about 30 percent of each fruit consists of healthful monounsaturated fat, which helps lower cholesterol. Its rich folate content helps prevent strokes. Avocados are also high in oleic acid (as is olive oil), which guards against breast cancer. What else? Evidently certain nutrients are absorbed more effectively when avocados are part of a meal, and the fruit is a great source of vitamin E. It's no small wonder both Sheryl and I like these glorious little powerhouses of great flavor and good health.

Cashew Butter and Fruit "Caviar"

CHUCK: *What I love about this appetizer is how unexpected it is. The slightly tart fruit caviar—so called because the* texture *of the fruit-flavored tapioca resembles caviar—is served with homemade cashew butter. The result? Something like a very grownup peanut butter and jelly treat.* Serves 15 to 20

CASHEW BUTTER

2 cups roasted, unsalted cashews

1 teaspoon freshly squeezed lemon juice

1 teaspoon agave nectar

¼ teaspoon kosher salt

2 to 3 tablespoons vegetable or canola oil

FRUIT "CAVIAR"

3 cups sugar-free fruit juice, such as grape or apricot, preferably organic

½ cup uncooked tapioca pearls

30 to 40 melba toasts, crostini, or other small crackers

1. To make the cashew butter: In the bowl of a food processor fitted with the metal blade, pulse the cashews, lemon juice, agave nectar, and salt 2 to 3 times until the nuts are crumbled and starting to form a paste.

2. With the processor running, drizzle the oil into the nut mixture until it comes together into a smooth butter. This won't be as smooth as creamy peanut butter but will have a little texture. If the butter is very thick, add a little water through the feed tube with the motor running, 1 teaspoon at a time. You should have about 2 cups of nut butter.

3. To make the caviar: In a small saucepan, bring the juice to a boil over medium-high heat. Reduce the heat to medium-low and simmer the juice until the amount reduces by a third, 7 to 8 minutes. When the juice is reduced to 2 cups, its flavor will be more intense.

4. Meanwhile, in another saucepan, bring 2 quarts (8 cups) of water to a boil over medium-high heat. Add the tapioca and cook until softened and transparent, about 20 minutes. If you see a small white spot in the middle of the mass, it will soon disappear when the tapioca is removed from the heat.

5. Transfer the tapioca to a colander to drain for 30 to 45 seconds (do not press on the tapioca with a spoon or it will turn into mush). When as much liquid as possible has drained, transfer the tapioca to a container with a tight-fitting lid. Pour the warm juice into the tapioca and stir to mix. Cover and refrigerate for at least 8 hours or overnight.

6. To serve, spread about 1 teaspoon of cashew butter on melba toasts or crostini and top with about 1 teaspoon of the fruit caviar.

RACHEL'S TIP

Not all canola oils are built the same. Look for organic, expeller-pressed oil to avoid chemical solvents and the potential presence of pesticide residues. Canola is ideal for high-heat cooking and has a neutral flavor.

Fried Green Tomato "BLT"

CHUCK: *I came up with this recipe one Saturday when I was cruising the farmers' market, looking for something to cook for Sheryl and some of her friends that evening. The tomatoes were at their peak, and so I decided to create an all-tomato meal. (I even picked up some tomato-strawberry ice cream.) This is a play on the classic BLT, but without the bread. I serve it as an appetizer, but it's a salad that serves as a light meal, too. If you want to go vegan, use Smart Bacon and instead of the aioli, use vegan mayo jazzed up with lemon juice and garlic powder.* Serves 4

EMULSION
½ cup seeded and diced very ripe
  tomatoes
Kosher salt and freshly ground black
  pepper
2 teaspoons truffle oil
1 teaspoon extra-virgin olive oil

BLT
8 slices pancetta, thick-cut, nitrate-
  free turkey bacon, or Smart Bacon
2 cups unbleached all-purpose flour
Kosher salt and freshly ground black
  pepper

4 large eggs, preferably omega-3 eggs
3 tablespoons milk
1½ cups whole-wheat flour
1 cup cornmeal
Eight ¼-inch-thick green tomato
  slices
Canola oil, preferably expeller-
  pressed, for frying

ASSEMBLY
4 to 5 tablespoons Roasted Garlic
  Aioli, page 29
3 cups baby spinach or arugula
  leaves

1. To make the emulsion: In a blender, pulse the tomatoes with salt and pepper to taste, 3 or 4 times or until smooth.
2. In a small bowl, combine the truffle and olive oils and slowly drizzle the oils into the blender through the feed tube while the blender is on medium speed. Pour the emulsion into a glass or plastic container, cover, and keep at room temperature.
3. To make the BLTs: Preheat the oven to 375°F.
4. Lay the pancetta slices on a baking sheet and cook for 8 to 10 minutes or until crispy. There is no need to turn the pancetta during oven cooking. Drain on paper towels and set aside.

5. In a shallow bowl, season the all-purpose flour lightly with salt and pepper. In another shallow bowl, whisk the eggs with the milk. In a third bowl, whisk together the whole-wheat flour and cornmeal and season lightly.

6. Toss the green tomato slices, 1 at a time, in the flour to coat on both sides. Dip them in the egg wash and coat them with the cornmeal mixture. Gently transfer the tomato slices to a plate or shallow pan lined with foil or parchment paper and lay them in a single layer without touching each other.

7. To fry, pour enough canola oil into a deep skillet to measure between $1/4$ and $1/2$ inch deep. Heat the oil over medium-high heat. The oil is hot enough for frying when the air directly above it shimmers. To test for doneness, drop a small cube of bread in the oil and if it sizzles and browns, the oil is ready. Another test is to sprinkle the oil with water to see if it will spatter and sizzle.

8. Fry the tomato slices, 1 or 2 at a time, in the hot oil, submerging them with long-handled tongs. Cook them, turning them once during frying, for 1 to 2 minutes or until golden brown on both sides. (Alternatively, fry the tomatoes in a deep-fat fryer.)

9. Transfer the fried tomatoes to a paper towel–lined platter or baking sheet and while warm, season lightly with salt and pepper. Set aside in a draft-free area of the kitchen or keep in the turned-off oven so that they don't cool too quickly.

10. To assemble: Put a tomato slice on a salad plate. Spread a teaspoon or so of aioli on top of the tomato and then top with a slice of pancetta. Put a small handful of spinach or arugula on the pancetta and then lay a second strip of pancetta over the greens. Top with another teaspoon or so of aioli and then with a second tomato slice and more greens. Drizzle the tomato emulsion over the greens and around the plate. Repeat to make 4 BLTs.

RACHEL'S TIP

Extra-virgin olive oil isn't the best choice for high-heat cooking. Compared to other oils it has a low smoke-point, and overheating releases carcinogens. For high-heat cooking with olive oil use extra-light or pure varieties.

Roasted Garlic Aioli

Makes about 1 ⅔ cups

2 large egg yolks

2 teaspoons chopped roasted garlic, see How to Roast Garlic on page 225

2 teaspoons freshly squeezed lemon juice

1 teaspoon Dijon mustard

1¼ cups light olive oil or canola oil, preferably expeller-pressed

Kosher salt and freshly ground black pepper

1. In the bowl of a food processor, pulse the egg yolks, garlic, lemon juice, and mustard several times until mixed.
2. With the motor running, slowly drizzle the oil through the feed tube until the aioli thickens to the consistency of a very light mayonnaise. Season to taste with salt and pepper.
3. Transfer the aioli to a container with a tight-fitting lid, cover, and refrigerate for up to 5 days.

RACHEL'S TIP

Egg yolks contain choline, which may reduce breast cancer risk, and lutein, which supports eye health.

Grilled Pimento Cheese Sandwiches with Roma Tomato Soup Shooters

CHUCK: *Forget about the pimento cheese sold in those small glass jars in the supermarket. With this recipe, you make it yourself. And it tastes intensely amazing. The combo brings back memories of classic lunches when I was a kid and my mom made tomato soup and grilled cheese sandwiches. You may not be familiar with pimento cheese sandwiches—I think pimento cheese is a Southern thing—but I make it with three kinds of cheeses from all parts of the country, so it's immediately universal. I serve the sandwiches with a fancy little soup shooter dressed up with truffle oil to make it a party. Plastic or glass shot glasses are sold in party supply stores. And speaking of parties, this is not an everyday grilled cheese sandwich, simply because there is a lot of fat in the homemade pimento cheese. So save it for those times when you crave a grilled cheese sandwich extraordinaire.* Serves 4

PIMENTO CHEESE

¾ pound sharp cheddar cheese, grated

½ pound smoked Gouda, grated

½ pound Colby Jack, grated

⅓ cup light mayonnaise

One 4-ounce can pimentos, drained and diced

2 tablespoons finely chopped cocktail-size pimento-stuffed olives

2 teaspoons olive juice (from the olives)

1 teaspoon garlic powder

1 teaspoon onion powder

1 teaspoon freshly ground black pepper

Kosher salt

2 to 3 tablespoons unsalted butter or soy butter, softened

8 slices sourdough bread

1 recipe Roma Tomato Soup with Truffle Oil, page 46

1. To make the cheese: In a large mixing bowl, mix together the cheddar, Gouda, and Jack cheeses. Fold in the mayonnaise, pimentos, olives, olive juice, garlic powder, onion powder, and pepper. Season to taste with salt.

2. Cover and refrigerate for at least 30 minutes to firm up a little, and up to 1 week. Stir well before serving.

3. To make the sandwiches: Lightly butter each slice of bread. Spread the pimento cheese on 4 slices of the bread and top with the remaining 4 slices.

4. In a large, nonstick skillet set over medium-high heat, grill the sandwiches until nicely browned on each side, 2 to 3 minutes on each side. As they cook, press gently on the sandwiches with a metal spatula.

5. To serve, cut the crusts off the bread and cut each sandwich into 4 triangles. Ladle the soup into 2- to 3-ounce shot glasses (you might want to use a funnel for this). Serve with the sandwiches on the side.

RACHEL'S TIP

What makes sourdough bread so delicious is also what makes it nutritious: the lactic acid, which will prevent blood sugars from spiking dramatically. That makes sourdough a much better option than other white breads.

Zucchini Muffins

SHERYL: *The first time Wyatt had one of Chuck's zucchini muffins it was as if he'd died and gone to muffin heaven. I was thrilled, of course, because I knew he was actually eating zucchini without the fuss factor. Now, the first thing out of his mouth every morning is, "I want a keenie muffin!" Being the creature of habit that he is, I believe he would start every day with one of Chuck's muffins, and the nice thing about it is that Mommy can make them, too!* Makes 12 muffins

2 large eggs, preferably omega-3 eggs, beaten

⅓ cup packed light brown sugar

2 teaspoons pure vanilla extract

3 cups grated fresh zucchini

⅔ cup canola oil, preferably expeller-pressed, plus more for greasing the muffin tins

2 teaspoons baking soda

½ teaspoon salt

3 cups unbleached all-purpose flour

2 teaspoons ground cinnamon

½ teaspoon ground nutmeg

1 cup chopped pecans

1 cup golden raisins

1. Preheat the oven to 350°F.
2. In a large bowl, whisk together the eggs, brown sugar, and vanilla. Stir in the grated zucchini, canola oil, baking soda, and salt.
3. In a separate bowl, whisk the flour with the cinnamon and nutmeg. Add the dry ingredients to the zucchini mix and stir well. Finally, stir in the pecans and raisins.
4. Grease a 12-cup muffin tin with canola oil. Spoon the batter into the cups to fill them about ¾ of the way. Bake for 25 to 30 minutes or until a toothpick or small knife inserted in a muffin comes out clean. (Alternatively, spoon the

batter into a 8 x 5 x 3-inch loaf pan. Bake for 50 to 55 minutes or until the top of the loaf cracks and a toothpick or small knife inserted in the center of the loaf comes out clean.)

5. Transfer the pan to a wire rack to cool for about 20 minutes. Then run a small paring knife around each muffin and remove them from the muffin tin.

RACHEL'S TIP

It's easy to flub oil storage, which results in a loss of flavor and nutrients. Even if stored under perfect conditions, many of the oil's properties degrade entirely after only 12 months. To keep your oil healthful, flavorful, and safe, follow these rules:
- Don't buy more oil than you'll use in six months.
- Buy oils in tinted glass to protect against light exposure.
- Pick bottles from the back of the shelf—again, less exposure to light.
- Store oil in a cool, dark place or refrigerate after opening—less exposure to light . . . you get the point!

Watermelon Margaritas

CHUCK: *These pretty, festive drinks are great in the summer when the melons are at their best. I first had them at Sheryl's, made by Chuck Coorts, her farm manager. I was blown away by them and while I tweaked the recipe a little, the credit goes to the "other" Chuck.* Serves 4

4½ cups peeled, diced seedless watermelon

¾ cup high-quality tequila (I prefer Patrón Silver tequila)

¼ cup sugar

¼ cup freshly squeezed lime juice

2 tablespoons triple sec

4 cups ice

1. In a blender, process half the watermelon, half the tequila, 2 tablespoons of sugar, 2 tablespoons of lime juice, 1 tablespoon of triple sec, and 2 cups of ice until smooth. Transfer to a pitcher.
2. Repeat with the remaining watermelon, tequila, sugar, lime juice, triple sec, and ice. Add this second batch to the first and refrigerate until ready to serve.

Soups

Cold Avocado-Cucumber Soup

CHUCK: *This is an easy soup to make and perfect on steamy, hot days because you literally don't have to go near the stove. All you need are ripe (but not too mushy) avocados and cucumbers from the garden or the local farm stand. When we're in Nashville, I can pick cucumbers from Sheryl's vegetable garden, which means they are super fresh. Add a little cilantro, and you're good to go. With its vibrant green color, the soup looks and is healthy and inviting. This is also an ideal recipe for those tricky times when I have to cook in a makeshift kitchen at a concert venue, often housed in a tent and with no "real" stove or refrigerator.*

Be sure to blend the soup long enough so that the cukes and avocados puree nicely. I work with a large blender and so can usually make all the soup at one time, but you might want to make this in two batches and stir it together at the end. Serves 6

> 3 ripe avocados, peeled, pitted, and coarsely chopped
>
> 2 medium-to-large cucumbers, peeled and coarsely chopped
>
> About 3 tablespoons coarsely chopped cilantro (about ⅓ bunch)
>
> Juice of 2 limes
>
> 3 teaspoons ground cumin
>
> 2 teaspoons garlic powder
>
> 2 teaspoons green Tabasco sauce
>
> Kosher salt and freshly ground black pepper

1. Put the avocados, cucumbers, cilantro, lime juice, and about ½ cup of water in a blender and process for 3 to 4 minutes or until smooth. (If the ingredients do not immediately start to liquefy, push on them gently with a rubber spatula to redistribute them in the blender.) Add the cumin, garlic powder, and Tabasco and blend for 2 or 3 minutes. Add more water, if needed, for the right consistency. Season to taste with salt and pepper.

2. Transfer the soup to a glass, ceramic, or other nonreactive bowl. Stir gently to mix, cover, and refrigerate for at least 2 hours and up to 24 hours. Taste and adjust the salt and pepper before serving.

Grilled Sweet Corn Soup with Garlic Popcorn

CHUCK: *When the corn is at its best in the summer, I like to cook it as often as I can—and in as many ways as possible. Luckily, Sheryl agrees. I grill the whole ears to give the soup a slight smokiness, and then simmer the stripped cobs in the stock to maximize the flavor.* Serves 4 to 6

SOUP

4 ears sweet corn, husked

2 tablespoons canola oil, preferably expeller-pressed

Kosher salt and freshly ground black pepper

1 medium-size yellow onion, diced

½ tablespoon chopped garlic

3 cups low-sodium chicken stock, preferably organic

1½ cups skim milk, preferably organic

2 sprigs fresh thyme or 1 teaspoon dried thyme

2 bay leaves

GARLIC POPCORN

3 tablespoons unsalted butter

1 teaspoon finely chopped garlic

2 tablespoons canola oil

½ cup unpopped popcorn kernels

4 to 6 tablespoons Crème Fraîche, page 153

1. Prepare a gas or charcoal grill so that the heating elements or charcoal are medium-hot. Before you start the fire, rub the grate with a little canola oil to prevent sticking.
2. To prepare the soup: Put the ears of corn in a large bowl. Add 1 tablespoon of the oil, and salt and pepper to taste, and roll the ears of corn in the oil to coat well.
3. Remove the corn from the bowl and grill for 6 to 8 minutes, turning the ears every 2 minutes so that they char lightly on all sides. Remove the corn from the grill and set aside to cool. When cool, hold the ears of corn upright over a plate or cutting board and using a sharp knife, slice the kernels from the cobs. Reserve the cobs.

4. In a large saucepan, heat the remaining tablespoon of oil over medium heat and when hot, add the onion and garlic and sauté slowly for 2 to 3 minutes or until the onion is translucent.

5. Add the chicken stock and milk, stir well, and bring to a boil before reducing the heat and bringing it down to a medium-low simmer. Adjust the heat up or down to maintain a gentle simmer. You do not want the soup to boil.

6. Add the cobs, thyme, and bay leaves to the saucepan. You may have to break the cobs in half to make them fit. Return the soup to a simmer and cook for 20 to 25 minutes. Remove the corn cobs, thyme sprigs, and bay leaves and discard.

7. Add the corn kernels to the soup and bring to a simmer. Cook for about 25 minutes longer, adjusting the heat to maintain a simmer and stirring occasionally. Let the soup cool for 10 to 15 minutes.

8. To make the popcorn: In a small microwave-safe dish, microwave the butter and garlic for about 30 to 50 seconds on medium power (depending on the microwave) or until melted. Remove the dish from the microwave and stir the contents to mix. Cover to keep warm. (Alternatively, melt the butter with the garlic in a small saucepan over medium-low heat.)

9. In a large, heavy pot with a tight-fitting lid, heat the canola oil over medium-high heat until hot but not smoking. Add the popcorn, cover tightly, and gently shake the covered pot for 2 to 3 minutes as the corn pops. Depending on the size of the pan and the heat of the flame, the corn may take a few minutes longer to pop, When the corn stops popping, remove the pot from the heat. Drizzle the popped corn with the warm garlic butter and set aside to cool for 5 to 10 minutes.

10. Ladle about half the soup into a blender and blend for 3 to 4 minutes or until very smooth. Transfer the blended soup to a large pot while you blend the remainder of the soup until smooth. Combine the blended soup; season to taste with salt and pepper. Return the soup to the saucepan and heat gently over medium heat until hot.

11. Ladle the hot soup into bowls and serve, garnished with a handful of popcorn and a swirl of crème fraîche.

Spring Pea and Mint Soup with Scallop Ceviche

SHERYL: *I have the most vivid memories of sitting around the coffee table with my two older sisters and my mom shucking peas when I was little. My mother and father shared a co-op vegetable garden with a few other neighbors when I was growing up, and we ate from it all summer long—big juicy tomatoes, squash, beans, lettuce, and of course peas. Chuck makes this soup for the band and me, and it's one of my favorites.* Serves 4 to 6

SCALLOP CEVICHE

About ¾ cup freshly squeezed lime juice (6 to 8 limes)

8 ounces scallops, diced small (⅛ to ¼ inch square; do not chop)

¼ cup diced red bell pepper

¼ cup diced poblano pepper

¼ cup diced red onion

2 tablespoons chopped scallions, white and green parts

1 tablespoon chopped cilantro leaves

1 teaspoon agave nectar

¾ teaspoon sea salt

½ teaspoon freshly ground black pepper

½ teaspoon chopped garlic

1 tablespoon olive oil

SOUP

1½ teaspoons olive oil

1 medium onion, diced

3 cups vegetable broth, preferably homemade

1 pound fresh or frozen shelled organic peas

⅓ cup chopped mint leaves

2 teaspoons freshly squeezed lemon juice

1½ teaspoons sugar

1½ teaspoons kosher salt

1 teaspoon freshly ground white pepper

1½ cups packed fresh spinach leaves

1. To prepare the ceviche: In a small glass or ceramic bowl, pour the lime juice over the scallops. There should be enough lime juice to cover them; if not, squeeze more limes until there is. Cover the bowl with plastic wrap and refrigerate for at least 6 hours and up to 8 hours or overnight.

2. Drain most of the lime juice from the scallops and transfer them to a larger glass or ceramic bowl. Add the bell pepper, poblano pepper, red onion, scallions, cilantro, agave nectar, salt, black pepper, and garlic. Toss gently. Drizzle with the olive oil, toss again, cover, and refrigerate for at least 2 hours and up to 2 days.

3. To make the soup: In a medium saucepan, heat the olive oil over medium heat. When hot, add the onion and sauté until softened, 3 to 4 minutes. Add the vegetable broth and bring to a boil.

4. Add the peas and the mint and cook for 4 to 5 minutes. Turn the heat to low and add the lemon juice, sugar, salt, and white pepper. Whisk the soup to mix all the ingredients, and then remove from heat. Let the soup cool for about 10 minutes.

5. Working in 2 batches and using a blender, puree half of the soup with half of the raw spinach for 2 to 3 minutes, then repeat with the other batch. Taste and adjust the seasoning, return the soup to the pot, and heat gently. If you are not ready to serve right away, turn the temperature to low, cover, and keep warm until serving.

6. Ladle the soup into shallow soup bowls and garnish each serving with about 2 tablespoons of the ceviche.

RACHEL'S TIP

Mint not only refreshes your senses, it also stimulates digestion.

CEVICHE SAVVY

I make ceviche most often with scallops, although shrimp is a good substitute. It's also excellent with firm-fleshed white fish, such as flounder, cod, or halibut. It's most important to begin with fresh, fresh fish that has no lingering odor but smells faintly briny, like the ocean. Try to find a merchant you can trust. Even the guy behind the counter at the super-market will be helpful, and it's worth your time to develop a relationship with him. He will tell you what's fresh!

The trick is to dice the fish or seafood with a sharp knife and take a little care to cut it into clean little cubes, not raggedy, chopped pieces. Not only is this neater, the fish will "cook" more evenly in the lime juice. And cook it does. The acid in the lime breaks down the protein in the fish or seafood, just as heat does, firming the flesh as it becomes opaque.

Roma Tomato Soup with Truffle Oil

CHUCK: *Sheryl is not a huge fan of tomatoes but we both recognize how healthful they are and so I serve them with some frequency. Lycopene, a carotenoid found in tomatoes, has impressive antioxidant properties, protecting cells and fighting cancer. Tomatoes are also packed with vitamin C. Research shows that organic tomatoes are more beneficial than others, and so whenever possible, I try to buy them from farm stands that boast organic, heirloom, or sustainably grown tomatoes.*

I sometimes serve this soup as a "shooter" with the pimento sandwiches (page 30), or another grilled cheese sandwich. If you're a tomato soup fan, by all means ladle the soup into larger bowls and dig in. And if you don't have or don't want to use the truffle oil, the soup is good without it. Serves 2 to 4

Note: You can stretch the truffle oil by mixing equal parts truffle oil and vegetable or canola oil. Very little flavor is lost and by doubling the amount of oil, you save money.

5 ripe Roma tomatoes, halved

2 tablespoons canola oil, preferably expeller-pressed, plus
    more for brushing the tomatoes

1 medium onion, sliced

1 tablespoon chopped garlic

2 tablespoons organic tomato paste

1 cup vegetable broth

One 12-ounce can diced tomatoes, preferably organic

1 cup tomato juice, preferably organic

1½ teaspoons sugar

1 bay leaf

Kosher salt and freshly ground black pepper

1½ tablespoons truffle oil, or more if desired

1. Prepare a gas or charcoal grill so that the heating elements or charcoal are medium-hot. Before you start the fire, rub the grate with a little canola oil to prevent sticking. (Alternatively, heat a countertop grill.)

2. Brush the tomato halves with a little olive oil. Grill them until nicely charred on both sides and softened, 2 to 3 minutes on each side. Use a thin metal spatula to turn them so they don't break. Set aside on a plate until needed.

3. In a deep, medium-size saucepan, heat the 2 tablespoons of oil over medium heat. When hot, cook the onion until softened, 3 to 4 minutes. Add garlic and cook, stirring, for 2 to 3 minutes longer. Take care the garlic does not burn.

4. Add the tomato paste, stir well, and cook for an additional 1 to 2 minutes. Add the vegetable broth and stir with a wooden spoon, scraping the pan to dislodge any onions sticking to the bottom. Bring the liquid to a low boil. Add the grilled tomatoes, canned tomatoes, and tomato juice and bring back to a simmer. When the soup is simmering, add the sugar and bay leaf and season to taste with salt and pepper. Simmer for 20 to 25 minutes or until the soup is well blended and flavorful. Remove the soup from the heat, and remove and discard the bay leaf.

5. Using an immersion blender, puree the soup until smooth, 2 to 3 minutes. With the blender running, slowly drizzle the truffle oil down the shaft of the blender to emulsify. Taste and add more oil if desired, 1 teaspoon at a time. (Alternatively, puree the soup in a blender and drizzle the oil into it through the lid. You may have to do this in 2 batches.)

6. Serve right away. If necessary, reheat gently until hot.

Veggie Caponata Soup

SHERYL: *This is one of Chuck's creations and there is not another soup like it. It is truly innovative and yummy at the same time. As he does with the Hummus Soup (page 157), he bases this soup on a popular spread. Caponata spread is made with eggplant and other garden vegetables such as tomatoes, squash, and onions, and then energized with capers, garlic, and often olives. So is the soup. It is bright tasting and just plain delicious.* Serves 8 to 10

3 tablespoons canola oil, preferably expeller-pressed

1 cup diced celery

1 medium red onion, diced

1 tablespoon chopped garlic

3 tablespoons tomato paste, preferably organic

4 cups vegetable broth

2 cups sliced crimini mushrooms

1½ cups diced zucchini

1½ cups diced eggplant

2 cups tomato juice, preferably organic

2 cups diced fresh tomatoes

½ cup chopped green olives

3 tablespoons drained capers

1 tablespoon freshly squeezed lemon juice

1½ teaspoons sugar

Kosher salt and freshly ground black pepper

2 cups packed arugula

½ cup chopped fresh basil leaves

1. In a large pot, heat the oil over medium-high heat until shimmering. When hot, add the celery, onion, and garlic and cook until they begin to soften, 2 to 3 minutes. Add the tomato paste and cook, stirring, for about 2 minutes longer. Add ¼ cup of the broth and stir gently to prevent the vegetables or tomato paste from sticking to the bottom of the pan. Cook for about 2 minutes longer, or until the stock has evaporated.

2. Add the mushrooms, zucchini, and eggplant and cook, stirring, to soften slightly, 3 to 4 minutes. Add the remaining $3^3/_4$ cups of broth and the tomato juice, tomatoes, olives, capers, lemon juice, and sugar. Season to taste with salt and pepper. Bring to a boil, stirring occasionally, over medium-high heat. Reduce the heat so that the soup simmers and cook for 20 to 25 minutes or until the flavors blend. Adjust the heat up or down to maintain the simmer. Taste and adjust the salt and pepper.

3. Just before serving, scatter the arugula and basil leaves over the hot soup and let the leaves wilt slightly, 1 to 2 minutes. Ladle into bowls and serve.

Salads

Watermelon, Basil, and Feta Salad

CHUCK: *The first time I served this to Sheryl and the band, they were a little skeptical. Watermelon salad? Yes! It's totally refreshing, a tempting amalgam of sweet, salty, and tangy flavors. Most important is to find a sweet, juicy melon, which is not too hard in the spring and summer.* Serves 6 to 8

¼ cup extra-virgin olive oil

2 teaspoons sherry vinegar

Kosher salt and freshly ground black pepper

4 cups peeled, diced seedless watermelon, cut into ½- to 1-inch cubes

½ cup thinly sliced red onion

⅓ cup coarsely chopped pitted Kalamata olives

¼ cup thinly sliced basil leaves

½ cup crumbled feta cheese

1. In a small bowl, whisk together the olive oil and vinegar until blended. Season to taste with salt and pepper and set aside.
2. In a medium-size mixing bowl, gently toss the watermelon with the red onion, olives, and basil. Season to taste with salt and pepper. Drizzle the dressing over the watermelon.
3. Transfer the salad onto a serving platter and top with the feta cheese. Serve immediately.

Sheryl's Tuna Salad

CHUCK: *I named this tuna salad for Sheryl because she eats it for lunch just about every day we are on the road. I sometimes make a sandwich with good, hearty whole-wheat bread or she eats the tuna spread on some kind of crispy cracker. I usually make the Caprese Salad (page 56) every day, too. It's a delicious match with the tuna. I am careful to buy tuna with minimal amounts of mercury, if any.*

SHERYL: *Yes, and I can safely say, Chuck has saved me from eating the same old tuna sandwich every day by incorporating apples and parsley into the mix. It is not your standard, boring old tuna salad!* Serves 3 to 4

Two 3¾-ounce cans organic, dolphin-safe, wild albacore tuna, drained
    (I like Vital Choice or Wild Planet brands)
⅓ cup finely diced tart apples, such as Granny Smith
¼ cup finely diced celery
2 tablespoons Vegenaise or low-fat mayonnaise (I like Smart Balance brand)
1½ teaspoons finely chopped flat-leaf parsley
½ teaspoon freshly squeezed lemon juice
Salt and freshly ground black pepper

1. In a glass or rigid plastic bowl and using a fork, mix together the tuna, apples, celery, Vegenaise or mayonnaise, parsley, and lemon juice. Stir just to mix; this should not be mushy. Season to taste with salt and pepper.
2. Use the tuna salad right away or cover and refrigerate for up to 48 hours.

RACHEL'S TIP

One serving of tuna contains a hefty dose of vitamin D, which promotes optimal breast health and helps regulate calcium. Just shop smart and get low-mercury canned tuna.

Bulgur Wheat Salad

SHERYL: *If you can imagine it, I used to eat junk food in the dressing room before my shows. Anything from powdered sugar donuts to corn chips and commercially prepared tuna salad. When I think about it now, my stomach churns! And, although I always took pride in my physical shape, diligently working out every day, a Diet Coke and a handful of chips in the afternoon was not an unusual snack for me to have. Since Chuck has been orchestrating our pre-show snacks and meals, grain salads rank high on my list of good-for-me foods. They're filling, satisfying, and give me tons of energy for the physically challenging concert to come later in the evening. I love to perform, and when I use the word "challenging," I mean it's a workout!* Serves 6 to 8

1 cup medium-grain bulgur wheat	1½ tablespoons extra-virgin olive oil
1 bulb fennel, trimmed and diced	1 tablespoon freshly squeezed lemon
½ cup shredded carrot	juice
½ cucumber, seeded and diced	1 tablespoon chopped fresh dill
(scant ½ cup)	2 teaspoons ground sumac, optional,
⅓ cup chopped curly-leaf parsley	see Note
¼ cup raisins, preferably organic	Kosher salt and freshly ground black
6 ounces feta cheese, crumbled	pepper
2 tablespoons drained capers	

Note: Ground sumac tastes tangy and fruity and can be found in Middle Eastern markets.

1. Preheat the oven to 375°F.
2. In a medium bowl, submerge the bulgur in 2½ cups boiling water. Stir gently and then cover with plastic wrap or waxed paper and set aside for at least 30 minutes or until all the water has been completely absorbed.
3. Spread the fennel in a small roasting pan and roast until softened and lightly browned, 8 to 10 minutes. Set aside to cool.
4. In a mixing bowl, toss together the carrot, cucumber, parsley, raisins, feta cheese, capers, olive oil, lemon juice, dill, and sumac. Add the vegetables to the cooled bulgur wheat and toss well. Fold in the roasted fennel and season to taste with salt and pepper. Cover and refrigerate for at least 2 hours and up to 12. The salad keeps, well covered and refrigerated, for up to 3 days.

Caprese Salad

CHUCK: *This salad is about as traditional as can be—why mess with perfection? I could dress the salad up with different vegetables and perhaps another kind of cheese, but there's good reason caprese salad has long been a favorite both in Italy and here. Sheryl loves it and eats it practically every day during the summer tour as an accompaniment to tuna salad (page 53). Both are light, healthful, and full of good, clean flavors. The green fruity flavor of the oil picks up the tang of the tomatoes and cheese, and is offset by the rich vinegar reduction.* Serves 2 to 3

About 1 pound medium-size, ripe heirloom tomatoes (2 to 3 tomatoes)

8 ounces fresh mozzarella cheese, sliced about ¼-inch thick

6 to 8 cucumber slices

6 to 8 fresh basil leaves

Kosher salt and freshly ground black pepper

1 tablespoon extra-virgin olive oil

1½ teaspoons Balsamic Reduction

1. Cut the tomatoes into thin slices, each about ¼ inch thick.
2. On each serving plate, arrange the tomato, mozzarella, and cucumber slices. Tuck the basil leaves between the slices. (Alternatively, chop the basil into a chiffonade, or very small pieces, and sprinkle the basil over the salad.)
3. Season to taste with salt and pepper and then drizzle with the olive oil and Balsamic Reduction. Serve right away.

Balsamic Reduction

Makes about ¼ cup

1 cup high-quality balsamic vinegar

In a small saucepan, bring the vinegar to a boil over medium-high heat. Simmer the vinegar until it reduces by three-quarters, so that there is about ¼ cup left. Transfer the reduced vinegar to a lidded container and chill for at least 2 hours and for up to 3 weeks.

Roasted Potato Salad with Sweet Corn and Cider Vinegar

CHUCK: *This is an awesome potato salad, especially during the summer when potatoes are young and tender. There is no need to peel the potatoes, and in fact the rosy red peels just add to the pleasure of eating this. Made without mayonnaise, it's light, refreshing, and totally delicious, if not conventional.*

When I am on the road with Sheryl, I roast the corn in the oven, as described on page 60. It's by far the easiest way to deal with corn. Setting up a grill is a major production, especially when I am scrambling to get a meal ready in the hours before the concert. If you prefer to grill corn over charcoal, by all means, do so. You won't be disappointed. Here's a trick you might like once the corn is grilled: Insert the husked ear of corn in the tube of a Bundt pan and then scrape the kernels from the cob. They collect in the pan rather than skittering around a cutting board.

Serves 8 to 10

2½ pounds unpeeled Red Bliss potatoes, diced into pieces about ½ inch square

1 medium-size red onion, halved and thinly sliced

2 tablespoons canola oil, preferably expeller-pressed

Kosher salt and freshly ground black pepper

½ cup extra-virgin olive oil

⅓ cup apple cider vinegar

Kernels from 3 ears roasted corn (about 1½ cups), see Cooking Corn on page 60

1 cup diced celery

¾ cup sliced fresh basil

2 teaspoons garlic powder

1. Preheat the oven to 425°F.
2. In a large bowl, toss the diced potatoes with the onion and canola oil. Season with salt and pepper and then spread on a lightly greased baking sheet. Bake the potatoes for 20 to 25 minutes or until crispy and yet still fork-tender. Set aside to cool to room temperature.

3. In small bowl, whisk together the olive oil and vinegar.

4. Return the cooled potatoes to the bowl and add the corn, celery, basil, and garlic powder. Drizzle the vinaigrette over the vegetables and toss to coat well. Season to taste with salt and pepper.

5. Cover and refrigerate for at least 2 hours and up to 8 hours before serving. If you don't plan to serve the salad for 7 or 8 hours, add the basil after refrigerating to prevent it from turning brown.

COOKING CORN

To roast the corn, cover the unhusked ears with water and soak for 10 to 15 minutes. Lay the soaked ears of corn in a shallow pan and roast in a preheated 375°F oven for about 25 minutes or until the corn kernels are tender. Let the corn cool so that you can handle the ears, remove and discard the husks and silks, and slice the corn kernels off the cobs. Three ears of corn should yield about 1½ cups of kernels. If you have a little more, all the better!

If you prefer to grill the corn in the husks, go for it. Remove the silks first and then pull the husks back over the ears of corn and grill it for about 25 minutes or until the corn kernels are tender. Let the ears of corn cool and then proceed with the above instructions.

Heirloom Tomato Panzanella Salad

CHUCK: *Panzanella salad is a superb way to eat tomatoes—they marinate with cucumbers, peppers, onions, cheese, greens, fresh herbs, and chewy bread. The result is a bright-tasting, soul-satisfying salad underlined with the saltiness of black olives and capers. And it's a good make-ahead dish, which helps when we're corralling the band and others for supper before the show.* Serves 8 to 10

1 loaf Italian or sourdough bread, 20 to 24 inches long, torn into rough, bite-size pieces (4 to 5 cups), see Note

⅓ cup extra-virgin olive oil

2 tablespoons white balsamic vinegar

2 teaspoons garlic powder

Kosher salt and freshly ground black pepper

5 to 6 ripe tomatoes, preferably heirloom, cored and diced (about 4 cups)

1 medium-size cucumber, seeded and cut into half-moon slices

8 ounces fresh mozzarella cheese, thinly sliced

2 cups packed fresh arugula

¾ cup sliced fresh basil

½ cup diced yellow bell pepper

½ cup sliced red onion

½ cup chopped, pitted Kalamata olives

2 tablespoons drained capers

Note: Look for day-old bread at the bakery or market; often these loaves are marked down in price. Otherwise, let the loaf sit out overnight to turn slightly stale.

1. Preheat the oven to 350°F.
2. Spread the bread on a baking sheet and lightly toast for 7 to 8 minutes. Stir and turn the bread once or twice during baking to brown. Set aside to cool.
3. In a small bowl, whisk together the olive oil, vinegar, and garlic powder. Season to taste with salt and pepper.
4. In a large mixing bowl, toss together the toasted bread, tomatoes, cucumber, cheese, arugula, basil, bell pepper, onion, olives, and capers. Drizzle the vinaigrette over the salad and toss to coat ingredients evenly.
5. Cover and refrigerate for about 20 minutes. Toss again and then refrigerate for about 1 hour before serving. Toss again before serving.

Southern Cobb Salad

CHUCK: *This salad gets its Southern bona fides from the crispy cooked country ham, which is comparable to prosciutto and serrano. Yankees and others who may not be familiar with the intense flavor and chewy texture of country ham may be surprised when they taste it, but down South, we know it well. It's always consumed judiciously simply because it's so rich and salty.*

I like to serve this salad with tobacco onions, which are nothing more exotic than fried onions that have been coated with a paprika and flour mixture. Once they are cooked, they develop the same deep brown color as tobacco. The term was coined by their creator, chef Dean Fearing of Rosewood Mansion on Turtle Creek in Dallas, Texas, who first cooked them back in the 1980s. Serves 4 to 5

TOBACCO ONIONS

1 medium red onion, peeled and cut into thin rings (try not to break the rings)

1 cup buttermilk

1 cup unbleached all-purpose flour

1 teaspoon paprika

1 teaspoon garlic powder

1 teaspoon salt

1 teaspoon freshly ground black pepper

2 cups canola oil, preferably expeller-pressed

SALAD

8 ounces country ham, 3 to 4 slices, see Note

2 heads romaine lettuce, outer leaves removed and discarded, chopped

⅓ cup Buttermilk Dressing, page 73

12 to 15 hard-cooked quail eggs, peeled, or 4 to 5 hard-cooked large hen eggs, peeled and chopped

¾ cup halved cherry tomatoes

6 ounces Tennessee cheddar cheese, or any good, local cheddar cheese, shredded (about 1 cup)

Note: Down South where Sheryl and I live, country ham is sold in 1-pound packages, with 6 to 8 slices of salty country ham. If you cannot find it, substitute Smart Bacon or another organic bacon.

1. To make the onions: Put the onion rings in a shallow bowl and cover with the buttermilk.

PRIDE OF THE SOUTH:
COUNTRY HAM

Country ham is a type of cured ham traditionally produced in Virginia following age-old techniques. Many small companies around the South cure country hams with sublime results; one of my favorites is Benton's Hams (bentonshams.com), which is located in my home state of Tennessee. As far as I am concerned, they make the best swine anyone could eat, hands down. No competition!

Country ham is cured in salt or brine and then smoked or dried. Once cured (which takes months and months), the hams must be soaked, the outer mold scraped off, and then cooked. Famed Southern cook Edna Lewis wrote in her book In Pursuit of Flavor *that before the hams are soaked they look "as though they have been buried." These days, most of us in the South buy our hams already cooked, although some folks still like to soak and cook them.*

2. In a shallow dish, whisk together the flour, paprika, garlic powder, salt, and pepper.
3. Lift the onion rings from the buttermilk and dip in the flour mixture to coat evenly.
4. Meanwhile, in a heavy, medium-size pot or large saucepan, heat the oil over medium-high heat to a temperature of 350°F, as registered on a deep-fat fryer thermometer or candy thermometer. Line a plate with several layers of paper towels and set it close to the stove.
5. Working in 2 batches, fry the onions until golden brown, 1½ to 2 minutes. Using tongs, remove the onion rings from the oil and let them drain on the paper towel–lined plate. Season with salt while still hot.
6. To make the salad: Preheat the oven to 350°F.
7. Spread the ham on a baking sheet and bake until crispy, 10 to 12 minutes. When cool, chop the ham so that you have ⅓ to ½ cup.
8. In a large mixing bowl, toss the chopped romaine with 2½ to 3 tablespoons of the buttermilk dressing.
10. Divide the salad evenly among 4 or 5 plates. Top each with quail eggs (or chopped hen eggs) and 6 to 7 tomato halves. Top the salads with country ham, cheese, and tobacco onions and serve immediately.

RACHEL'S TIP

Healthful oils aren't just an option, they are a requirement with your antioxidant-rich, super-protective veggies. Adding a touch of oil to any salad will maximize your nutrient absorption.

WHY I BUY ORGANIC PRODUCE WHENEVER I CAN

Food scientists have identified the so-called "dirty dozen" foods to avoid when raised conventionally. In other words, buy these organic whenever possible. Even better, buy them from a farmer you know and trust (like the guy at the farmers' market who is only too happy to talk to you about his farming methods).

Ready? Let me introduce you to these bad boys: apples, celery, cherries, imported grapes, lettuce, nectarines, peaches, pears, potatoes, sweet bell peppers, spinach, and strawberries. Because these foods tend to be delicate and susceptible to insect invasions, conventional farmers douse them with pesticides, which cling to them even in the supermarket. You can't see them or smell them, but trust me. They are there.

Regardless of how they are grown, all fruits and veggies should be washed with cool, running water, but these (if raised conventionally) should be given an extra dunk. And by the way, fresh, cool water is all you need to clean produce; those "washes" don't really do anything.

Roasted Vegetable and Quinoa Pasta Salad

CHUCK: *Summer vegetables such as zucchini, yellow squash, and asparagus roast quickly and are delicious when tossed with nutty quinoa "pasta." If you haven't tried pasta made from quinoa, don't wait another day. It's so delicious you'll forget it's so healthful. For more on quinoa, turn to page 96.* Serves 6 to 8

1 bunch asparagus, tough stem ends removed, cut into 1-inch-long pieces

1 cup diced zucchini (1 zucchini)

1 cup diced yellow squash (1 small squash)

1 medium-size red onion, diced

2 teaspoons garlic powder

1 tablespoon canola oil, preferably expeller-pressed

Kosher salt and freshly ground black pepper

2 teaspoons maple syrup

2 teaspoons apple cider vinegar

½ teaspoon Dijon mustard

2 teaspoons chopped fresh basil leaves

1 teaspoon chopped fresh dill

1 teaspoon chopped fresh tarragon

¼ cup olive oil

4 cups cooked quinoa pasta (I like Ancient Harvest's Veggie Curls or Garden Pagodas)

2 cups loosely packed fresh spinach

½ cup diced roasted red peppers, preferably organic (from a jar or see page 101 for how to roast your own)

1. Preheat the oven to 400°F. Line 2 baking sheets with aluminum foil or spray them lightly with canola oil spray.

2. In a large bowl, toss together the asparagus, zucchini, squash, and onion. Sprinkle with the garlic powder and canola oil and toss to coat. Season to taste with salt and pepper.

3. Spread the vegetables evenly on the baking sheets and roast until softened but

still firm, 10 to 12 minutes. Set the baking sheets aside and let the vegetables cool.

4. Meanwhile, whisk together the maple syrup, vinegar, mustard, basil, dill, and tarragon. Season to taste with salt and pepper and then slowly whisk in the olive oil.

5. In a large mixing bowl, toss the roasted vegetables with the pasta, spinach, and red peppers. Drizzle the dressing over the salad, tossing to mix thoroughly. Cover the bowl or transfer the salad to a glass container with a lid and refrigerate for at least 12 hours before serving. The salad will keep for 2 to 3 days.

RACHEL'S TIP

How you cook your pasta matters. Slightly firm, or al dente pasta keeps your blood sugar steady. Your best bet? Shaped pastas, which are easier to cook al dente (particularly compared to narrow strand pastas such as angel hair), and allow more lycopene-rich marinara sauce to cling to them.

Iceberg Wedge Salad with Cumin-Lime Vinaigrette

CHUCK: *Nowadays, iceberg wedge salads are all the rage—a play on the pale-green wedge salads served in old-time steak houses, doused with blue cheese dressing. I use a mild farmer cheese for my salad and team it with grapefruit and jicama. Drizzled with the lime-based dressing, it's light, refreshing, and always welcome. Plus, it's easy to make: Nothing is easier than cutting heads of iceberg lettuce into quarters. You may have given up on iceberg lettuce—but give it another chance, especially if you buy it from a farmer or at a farmers' market. These heads tend to have marginally more nutrients than the heads of iceberg sold in supermarkets, but regardless of its source, iceberg lettuce does not rank high in vitamins and minerals. To combat that, you could make this salad with romaine or another crunchy green instead.* Serves 4

> 2 large grapefruits
> 1 head iceberg lettuce, quartered and cored
> 4 ounces Cotija or firm farmer cheese, crumbled
> ½ cup grated jicama root
> ¼ cup toasted pumpkin seeds
> About ¼ cup Cumin-Lime Vinaigrette, page 70

1. Peel the grapefruits. Holding them, one at a time, over a bowl or sink to catch the juices, separate them into segments. After segmenting both, you will have 20 to 24 segments. If you want, use the juice for another purpose.
2. Put a lettuce wedge on each of 4 serving plates or shallow salad bowls. Divide the cheese, jicama, pumpkin seeds, and grapefruit segments among the servings, and drizzle each serving with about 1 tablespoon of dressing.

Cumin-Lime Vinaigrette

CHUCK: *While I love this with the wedge salad on page 69, it would perk up a southwestern-style salad made with black beans, corn, bell peppers, red onion, and cilantro. Don't stop there. Use the vinaigrette to marinate fish, pork, or flank steak to fill tacos or make fajitas.* Makes about ½ cup

1 tablespoon freshly squeezed lime juice

1½ teaspoons ground cumin

1 teaspoon agave nectar

2 teaspoons sherry vinegar

Grated zest of 1 lime (about 1 teaspoon)

¼ cup canola oil, preferably expeller-pressed

Kosher salt and freshly ground black pepper

1. In a small glass or ceramic bowl, whisk together the lime juice, cumin, agave nectar, vinegar, and lime zest. Still whisking, slowly add the canola oil until the dressing is emulsified. Season to taste with salt and pepper. (Alternatively, make the dressing in a blender and add the oil through the feed tube with the blender running.)
2. Transfer the dressing to a container with a tight-fitting lid and refrigerate for up to 2 weeks. Whisk well before using.

Mâche Salad with Sherry Vinegar Gastrique

CHUCK: *Mâche is sold in just about every supermarket, but if you can't find salad greens called "mâche," don't be surprised. It's also called field salad, lamb's lettuce, and corn salad. Just about any mild spring or young greens mix will do, topped with roasted beets and a sweet-and-sour gastrique.* Serves 4

1 medium-sized beet, ends trimmed

2 to 3 carrots

1 tablespoon plus 1 teaspoon avocado oil or olive oil

Juice of ½ lemon

Kosher salt and freshly ground black pepper

5 cups mâche lettuce or tender mixed greens

⅔ cup halved cherry or grape tomatoes

2 medium-sized avocados, halved, pitted, and diced

About ¼ cup Sherry Vinegar Gastrique, page 72

1. Preheat the oven to 350°F.
2. Rinse the beet under cool water and then put the damp beet in a small roasting pan, cover, and roast for 45 to 60 minutes or until fork tender. Let the beet cool until you can handle it and then slip off the skins. They will come off easily. (If you wear latex gloves, your fingers won't turn pink.) Cut the beets into thin slices, no more than ¼-inch thick, and set aside.
3. Wash and peel the carrots. With a vegetable peeler, make lengthwise "ribbons" from the carrots by running the peeler along the length of the carrots. You need 16 to 20 carrot ribbons in all.
4. In a glass, ceramic, or other nonreactive mixing bowl, whisk together the avocado oil, lemon juice, salt and pepper.
5. Add the lettuce and toss to coat. Divide the lettuce among 4 small serving plates. Garnish each salad with 4 to 5 beet slices, 5 to 6 tomato halves, diced avocado, and 4 to 5 carrot ribbons.
6. Drizzle each salad with about 1 tablespoon of the gastrique and serve.

Sherry Vinegar Gastrique

CHUCK: *Try this with the mâche salad on page 71 and other salads and you will quickly realize how versatile gastriques are. Most commonly they are used to glaze meat and poultry, and when I do so, I often reserve a little of the gastrique to sprinkle over salad greens that accompany the meat. I also like to drizzle this one over fresh strawberries or creamy goat cheese to tweak their flavors. It's also a great glaze for sweet potatoes.* Makes about ½ cup

1 cup sherry vinegar

⅓ cup sugar

¼ teaspoon kosher salt

2 to 3 sprigs fresh thyme

2 to 3 fresh sage leaves

1 bay leaf

½ sprig fresh rosemary

½ teaspoon black peppercorns

1. In a small saucepan, combine the vinegar, sugar, and salt and bring to a boil over medium-high heat, stirring occasionally as the mixture heats. Let the mixture boil for 10 to 12 minutes or until reduced by half.

2. Reduce the heat to low so that the vinegar simmers. Stir in the thyme, sage, bay leaf, rosemary, and peppercorns and let the gastrique simmer for 3 to 4 minutes. Remove from the heat and set aside to cool for 10 minutes.

3. Strain the gastrique into a glass bowl and let it cool to room temperature. At this point, the gastrique should be the consistency of light syrup, and thick enough to coat the back of a spoon. Use right away or cover and store at room temperature for up to 10 days.

Buttermilk Dressing

CHUCK: *I love this dressing and nearly always have a jar of it in the refrigerator. It's great with the Cobb salad on page 63 and just about any leafy or chunky salad. I also spread it on sandwiches in place of mayonnaise and serve it as a dip for raw, garden-fresh vegetables.* Makes about 1 cup

⅓ cup buttermilk

⅓ cup light sour cream

⅓ cup light mayonnaise

1½ tablespoons apple cider vinegar

1 tablespoon chopped flat-leaf parsley

¾ teaspoon garlic powder

½ teaspoon onion powder

½ teaspoon sugar

Kosher salt and freshly ground black pepper

1. In a medium bowl, whisk together the buttermilk, sour cream, mayonnaise, vinegar, parsley, garlic powder, onion powder, and sugar until well combined. Season to taste with salt and pepper.
2. Pour the dressing into a container with a tight-fitting lid and refrigerate for up to 2 weeks.

Main Courses

Free-Range Organic "Airliner" Chicken Breasts

SHERYL: *Like the rest of America, we eat a lot of chicken. Just about everyone likes it, plus it can be prepared in so many ways. It's also pretty low in fat and calories. Chuck makes chicken fun and interesting by adding Corn and Thyme Pancakes, which gives the dish a very Southern flare.* Serves 4

Note: Airliner chicken breasts halves are thick, bone-in chicken breasts, with the skin on. The term was popularized in the 1960s when the airlines served chicken breast halves with the wing still attached. The wing made the relatively small cut of chicken look bigger.

2 tablespoons freshly squeezed lemon juice

⅓ cup olive oil

4 airliner chicken breast halves, see Note

About ¾ cup roughly torn or chopped fresh herbs, including stems, such as rosemary, thyme, tarragon, and sage

4 Corn and Thyme Pancakes, page 111

4 cups Mâche Salad, page 71

4 or 5 tablespoons Sherry Vinegar Gastrique, page 72

1. In a small bowl, whisk together the lemon juice and olive oil. Coat the chicken liberally with the mixture and then put it in a shallow, nonreactive roasting pan or in a large, sealable plastic bag. Sprinkle with the herbs and turn the pieces several times to coat evenly, or turn the bag a few times to mix well. Refrigerate for at least 4 hours and up to 12 hours.

2. About 1 hour before cooking, lift the chicken breasts from the marinade and let any excess drip back into the pan or bag. Lay the chicken in a single layer in a shallow glass dish and cover with plastic wrap.

3. Preheat the oven to 400°F. In medium-large sauté pan set over medium-high heat, sear chicken breasts, skin side down, until golden brown, 3 to 4 minutes. Turn the chicken over and sear for 2 minutes longer. When seared, transfer the chicken breasts to a lightly oiled baking sheet or shallow pan and bake for about 20 minutes.

4. Put a pancake on each plate and top with about 1 cup of salad. Top each serving with a chicken breast and drizzle about a tablespoon of gastrique over each.

Mojo Criollo Slow-Braised Pork

CHUCK: *I don't know a single meat eater who doesn't swoon over slow-cooked pork. It's tender and full of flavor, picking up the intoxicating spices from south of the border. Like many long-cooking dishes, preparation is fast and easy, and it's the cooking itself that is time-intensive. I suggest making this in a disposable aluminum foil pan simply because after all this time in the oven, the pan drippings do a number on your shiny roasting pan, leaving it near impossible to clean. But of course, it's your choice. Don't forget to recycle the aluminum foil pan!* Serves 6 to 8

1 cup freshly squeezed lime juice

1 cup freshly squeezed orange juice

2 tablespoons chopped garlic

1 tablespoon dried oregano

2 teaspoons kosher salt

2 teaspoons freshly ground black pepper

1 teaspoon dried red chili flakes

1 teaspoon ground cumin

¾ cup canola oil, preferably expeller-pressed

1 bunch scallions, white and green parts, sliced

⅓ cup chopped fresh cilantro leaves

One 3- to 4-pound boneless Boston butt (pork shoulder), cut into 2 large pieces

12 ounces Mexican beer, such as Corona, Dos Equis, or Sol

1 recipe Sofrito Rice with Green Chiles and Mango, page 109

1. In a blender, process the juices, garlic, oregano, salt, pepper, chili flakes, and cumin. With the blender on medium speed, slowly drizzle canola oil through the opening in the lid. When the oil is absorbed and the marinade is nicely emulsified, remove the canister from the blender and stir in the scallions and cilantro.

2. Put the pork pieces in a glass, ceramic, or other nonreactive dish. Pour the marinade over the pork, cover, and refrigerate for at least 8 hours and up to 12 hours.

3. Preheat the oven to 250°F.

4. Transfer the pork to a disposable aluminum pan. Pour the marinade and the beer over the pork, cover tightly with aluminum foil, and braise until very tender, 6 to 7 hours. The pork is done when it just about falls apart when prodded with a fork. Keep cooking it until it's tender.

5. Shred the pork with 2 forks and your fingers. Serve with the rice.

Roasted Salmon with Blueberry BBQ Sauce

CHUCK: *Salmon is a great fish . . . period. It is high in omega oils, is not too fishy, and is usually easy to find in supermarkets and fish stores. Try to find wild-caught salmon instead of farm raised. Farmed salmon can contain as much as ten times the toxins as wild salmon, which is as good a reason as any to avoid it.*

I pair salmon with a vivid blueberry barbecue sauce to jazz up its buttery flavor with a little sweetness and tartness—plus the sauce gives me a chance to use blueberries. They're a great source of antioxidants and are considered a "super food" by many nutritionists. I like to pair this low-carbohydrate, high-protein dish with Grilled Asparagus and Red Peppers (page 100). There's no denying this is a dish best suited for a party or other special occasion; the sugar and honey paired with the rich salmon make it a delightful indulgence. Serves 4

2 teaspoons canola oil, preferably expeller-pressed

¼ cup diced onion

1 teaspoon chopped garlic

¼ cup ketchup, preferably high-fructose corn syrup–free

¼ cup white wine vinegar

4 tablespoons brown sugar

3 tablespoons Dijon mustard

2 teaspoons Worcestershire sauce

2 tablespoons honey

1 teaspoon dried red chili flakes

2 cups fresh blueberries

Kosher salt and freshly ground black pepper

Four 6- to 8-ounce center-cut salmon fillets, with the pin bones removed
   (each fillet should be 1 to 1½ inches thick)

1. In a small saucepan, heat the canola oil over medium-high heat and when hot, add the onions and sauté for 2 to 3 minutes or until slightly softened. Add the garlic and cook, stirring, for about 2 minutes longer, until fragrant. Reduce the heat to medium-low and stir in the ketchup, vinegar, brown sugar, mustard,

Worcestershire sauce, honey, and chili flakes. Cook until the sauce simmers.

2. Add the blueberries to the simmering sauce and cook for 10 minutes, adjusting the heat up or down to maintain the simmer. Stir frequently to keep the sauce fluid. Many of the berries will break open, which is okay.

3. Carefully transfer the hot sauce to the bowl of a food processor fitted with the metal blade and puree until smooth. Season to taste with salt and pepper. If the sauce is too thick, add water, 1 tablespoon at a time. Scrape the sauce into a container with a tight-fitting lid and set aside to cool to room temperature.

4. Preheat the oven to 400°F. Line a baking sheet with aluminum foil and coat the foil lightly with canola oil.

5. Season the salmon fillets with salt and pepper on both sides and then lay them on the baking sheet. Brush each fillet with a generous amount of the sauce. After you are through, clean the brush thoroughly under running water.

6. Bake the salmon for 5 minutes and then remove the baking sheet from the oven. With the clean brush, lather a generous amount of sauce over the fillets and bake for 3 to 5 minutes longer or until the fish is cooked through. (For medium-cooked salmon, reduce the cooking time by 2 to 3 minutes.) Serve drizzled with more sauce, if desired.

Marcona Almond–Dusted Scallops with Sweet Corn, Leeks, and Tomatoes

CHUCK: *I can't imagine summer without fresh tomatoes, sweet corn, and buttery scallops. Here, I pair scallops with Marcona almonds, which are raised without a lot of pesticides (see Why We Like Almonds on page 84). Try to buy what are called diver scallops, which are harvested by hand, or at the very least look for scallops that are creamy white or with a pink tinge. Avoid bright, pure-white scallops. These have been soaked in chemicals to lengthen their shelf-life, and while the soaking doesn't ruin them, it does diminish their flavor. I would buy flash-frozen scallops over fresh scallops that have been so treated any day. Today, most scallops have been trimmed of the little flap, or muscle, that attached them to the shell, but if you buy them with it still attached, pluck it off with your fingers.* Serves 4

> 12 to 14 extra-large scallops (U10 size), with side muscle removed, if necessary
> ½ cup shelled Marcona almonds
> 3 teaspoons canola oil, preferably expeller-pressed
> ½ cup diced leeks (white part only)
> 1 tablespoon chopped garlic
> Kernels cut from 3 to 4 medium-size ears corn, roasted (about 1½ cups),
>   see Cooking Corn on page 60
> ¼ cup white wine
> 1½ cups packed arugula leaves (about 2 generous handfuls)
> ¾ cup halved cherry tomatoes
> 1 tablespoon soy butter or unsalted butter
> Kosher salt and freshly ground black pepper
> Parsley Oil, page 85

1. Gently rinse the scallops under cool, running water and drain on a plate lined with paper towels. Refrigerate until ready to cook, but for no longer than 10 hours.
2. In the bowl of a food processor fitted with the metal blade, pulse the almonds

to a fine powder. Do not overprocess or the almonds will turn into almond butter. Set aside. (A mini food processor works very well here.)

3. In large sauté pan, heat 2 teaspoons of the canola oil over medium-high heat and when hot, cook the leeks and garlic for 2 to 3 minutes or until the leeks are translucent. Stir in the corn and cook for about 2 more minutes. Add the wine, bring to a boil, reduce the heat slightly, and simmer briskly for about 30 seconds to give it time to cook off. Use a wooden spoon to deglaze the pan by dislodging any bits of food stuck to the bottom.

4. Add the arugula, tomatoes, and butter to the pan and stir just to mix. Season to taste with salt and pepper and remove from the heat. Cover the pan to keep the vegetables warm while you cook the scallops.

5. Set a large sauté pan over high heat and while it heats, season the scallops with salt and pepper.

6. Add the remaining 1 teaspoon of canola oil to the pan and when it is hot and shimmering, gently put scallops in the pan and sear for 2 to 3 minutes without touching the scallops at all. Using tongs, flip the scallops over and immediately remove the pan from the heat. Leave the scallops in the hot pan for 2 to 3 minutes to allow the residual heat to cook them to perfection. They will be medium to medium-well done.

7. Spoon a generous amount of corn sauté in the middle of each of 4 plates. Top it with 3 or 4 scallops and sprinkle the scallops liberally with almond powder. Using a teaspoon, drizzle the parsley oil around the edge of the plates and serve.

RACHEL'S TIP

Parsley can freshen both your breath and your insides. A mild diuretic (which most girls appreciate before special events), parsley also contains cancer-fighting and anti-inflammatory properties.

WHY WE LIKE ALMONDS

When she's working, Sheryl often needs healthful snacks to keep her going. They have to taste great, work quickly, and not spoil her appetite for dinner. Almonds do it all! Almonds—which are drupe pits or seeds (think cherries, peaches, nectarines) and so not actually nuts—are packed with nutrients, monounsaturated fat, and extremely pleasing flavor. According to some research, almonds can significantly help lower LDL cholesterol if eaten regularly—just a handful a day does the job.

We especially like Marcona almonds because unlike most of the almonds sold in the United States, Spanish Marconas grow inside super-protective shells that naturally resist insects and disease and so may be cultivated naturally with no need for pesticides. A quarter cup of Marconas offers about 3 grams of fiber, 6 grams of protein, and noteworthy amounts of calcium, iron, and vitamin E. Sweet almonds are equally healthful. Whether you snack on Marcona or more ordinary sweet almonds, you will be rewarded with a satisfying and tasty snack.

Parsley Oil

CHUCK: *The magical part of making this parsley oil is that the longer you puree it, the greener it gets. Don't stop blitzing it after a minute or two, but let the blender do its thing for four to five minutes. Of course there is a tipping point, which means if you puree it for too long, the parsley will turn a little brown, so watch it carefully. It's also worth remembering that this is not a last-minute condiment but must be made well ahead of time because it needs to be strained for about 12 hours—or longer. Once it's strained and the pretty green, full-flavored oil is clear and bright, you can store it for a few weeks.* Makes about 1½ cups

> 2 to 3 tablespoons kosher salt, plus 1½ teaspoons
> 2 bunches flat-leaf parsley
> 1½ cups vegetable or canola oil

1. Fill a medium saucepan about three quarters full with water and stir 2 to 3 tablespoons of salt into the water. Fill a bowl with cold water and ice and set it next to the stove.
2. Bring the salted water to a boil over medium-high heat and holding the parsley bunches by the stems, dip the leafy parts in the water for 15 to 20 seconds to blanch. Immediately submerge the parsley into the ice water, remove, and pat dry with paper towels or a clean kitchen towel.
3. Cut the stems from the parsley bunches when they have been blanched.
4. In a blender, puree the parsley, oil, and about 1¹/₂ teaspoons of salt for 4 to 5 minutes or until smooth and bright green.
5. Line a strainer with a paper coffee filter and set the strainer over a glass bowl. Pour the parsley oil into the coffee filter and let the oil drain into the bowl, which can take as long as 12 hours.
6. Cover the bowl with plastic wrap and refrigerate for up to 2 weeks. Let the oil return to room temperature and liquefy before using.

Blue Corn Tortilla–Crusted Red Snapper with Margarita Butter

CHUCK: *I spike the butter sauce with a little tequila for a flavor jolt, but if you're not in the mood for boozy butter (and I say that with a nod and a wink because the butter isn't particularly alcoholic—a lot of the alcohol burns off during cooking), make a quick sauce with soy butter and freshly squeezed lime juice: 1 tablespoon of juice for 1 tablespoon of butter. Easy! And just as tasty with the snapper. The smooth butter is great with the slightly crunchy, breaded fish. When I discovered what a great "breading" crispy corn tortillas made, I looked around for ways to use them. The red snapper, with its mild yet distinctive flavor, is a perfect vehicle. The crunch complements the flaky white fish. Plus, we usually have a bag or two of blue corn chips in the portable, on-the-road pantry, and so it makes all kinds of sense.*

Serves 4

Note: To make the tortilla corn chip crumbs, process the corn chips in the bowl of a food processor fitted with the metal blade. For 1 cup of crumbs, you need 4 to 5 ounces of chips.

MARGARITA BUTTER

½ cup drinkable tequila (no rotgut stuff), plus 2 teaspoons

¼ cup freshly squeezed lime juice

¼ cup freshly squeezed orange juice

4 tablespoons soy butter or unsalted butter

Kosher salt and freshly ground black pepper

½ teaspoon agave nectar

RED SNAPPER

Four 6- to 7-ounce red snapper fillets, skin on or off

Kosher salt and freshly ground black pepper

2 tablespoons milk

1 large egg

1 cup finely ground blue corn tortilla chips, see Note

1 teaspoon ground cumin

1 teaspoon chili powder

1 teaspoon ground coriander

1 recipe Black Bean and Roasted Corn Sauté, page 107

1. To make the butter: In a small saucepan, combine the ½ cup of tequila, lime juice, and orange juice and set over medium-high heat. Bring the liquid to a boil and cook until reduced by two-thirds, 8 to 10 minutes.

2. Remove the pan from the heat and whisk in the soy butter, 1 tablespoon at a time. Season to taste with salt and pepper, the agave nectar, and the remaining 2 teaspoons of tequila. If the sauce is too bitter, add more agave, ¼ teaspoon at a time. Cover to keep warm until needed.

3. To make the snapper: Preheat the oven to 375°F. Season the fillets with salt and pepper.

4. In a small bowl, whisk together the milk and egg.

5. In another shallow bowl, stir together the tortilla chips, cumin, chili powder, and coriander.

6. Brush the top of each fillet with the egg wash and gently lay the snapper in the tortilla mixture, brushed side down (and skin side up, if the fillets have skin). Evenly coat the side of the fillet in the tortilla mixture. Transfer the fillets to a lightly greased baking sheet, coated sides up, and bake until cooked through, 8 to 10 minutes.

7. Serve each fillet with the Black Bean and Roasted Corn Sauté and drizzled with about 1 tablespoon of the butter sauce.

Pecan-Crusted Trout

SHERYL: *Before I met Chuck, I wasn't a big fish eater, but since he has joined me on the road, fish has figured a lot more into my diet. I appreciate this because of its myriad health properties: low in calories, high in omega-3 fatty acids and protein, and an excellent source of minerals and vitamins, such as niacin and vitamin B12. Trout is a great fish to cook because it's often easy to find locally caught or raised, and therefore super-fresh. It's also a low-mercury fish, which makes it a great choice.* Serves 4

¼ cup unbleached all-purpose flour

1 teaspoon lemon-pepper seasoning

½ teaspoon garlic powder

1 large egg

1½ tablespoons milk

1 cup chopped pecans

Four 4- to 5-ounce skin-on trout fillets

2 tablespoons canola oil, preferably expeller-pressed

1 recipe Edamame Succotash, page 102

1. Preheat the oven to 375°F.
2. In a shallow dish, whisk together the flour, seasoning, and garlic powder. In a second dish, whisk together the egg and milk. Put the pecans in a third dish or plate.
3. Coat the side of a fillet without the skin with the flour and then with the egg wash. Press it gently into the pecans to coat thoroughly. Repeat with the remaining trout fillets, so that all 4 are coated on the side without skin.
4. In a large skillet, heat the canola oil over medium-high heat and when hot, sear the trout, skin side up, for 2 minutes. Turn the fish fillets gently with a spatula and sear the skin side for 2 minutes longer. Transfer the fillets to a lightly oiled baking sheet or shallow pan and bake for 8 to 10 minutes or until cooked through. Serve the fish with the Edamame Succotash.

Asian-Marinated Tofu with Pea-Wasabi Coulis

CHUCK: *Sheryl and most of the band enjoy meat and fish, but I do have a few vegetarian main courses in my arsenal that I like to throw into the mix now and again. Marinated tofu is great—it takes on whatever flavors are mixed with it, and when it's firm and pressed, and then cooked, it has a pleasingly meaty texture. The pea coulis and grit cakes dress it up very smartly, both in terms of flavor and presentation.* Serves 4

TOFU

1-pound block extra-firm tofu, pressed, see Try Cooking with Tofu on page 18

1 tablespoon soy sauce

2 teaspoons rice vinegar

2 teaspoons freshly squeezed lime juice

1½ teaspoons ground ginger

1 teaspoon garlic powder

½ teaspoon dried red chili flakes

1½ teaspoons sesame oil

1½ tablespoons canola oil, preferably expeller-pressed

PEA COULIS

8 ounces thawed frozen peas (about 2 cups)

¼ cup vegetable stock

1½ teaspoons freshly squeezed lime juice

1½ teaspoons prepared wasabi paste, plus more if desired

¼ teaspoon white pepper

Kosher salt

1 recipe Carrot Relish, page 93

4 fresh scallions, trimmed, or cilantro sprigs, for garnish

4 Sesame-Shiitake Grit Cakes, page 112

1. To make the tofu: Cut the tofu into 4 equal-size portions. Put them in a shallow, nonreactive roasting pan or in a large, sealable plastic bag.

2. In a small bowl, whisk together the soy sauce, vinegar, lime juice, ground

ginger, garlic powder, and chili flakes. Gradually whisk in the sesame oil and then the canola oil until emulsified.

3. Pour the marinade over the tofu and turn the pieces several times to coat evenly, or turn the bag a few times to mix well. Refrigerate for at least 3 hours and up to 12 hours.

4. To make the coulis: In a blender, mix together the peas, stock, lime juice, wasabi paste, and white pepper and blend on medium speed until pureed, 2 to 3 minutes.

5. Taste and add more wasabi, if desired. Make sure the wasabi does not mask the flavor of the peas. Season to taste with salt.

6. Transfer to a saucepan, cover, and set over very low heat to take the chill off. If the kitchen is very warm and you have other burners going, the pan will probably warm up enough set on a switched-off burner. (Alternatively, cover and refrigerate for up to 3 days. Reheat in a saucepan or microwave before serving.)

7. Remove tofu from marinade and let any excess marinade drip back into the dish.

8. In a medium sauté pan set over medium-high heat, sear the tofu for about 3 minutes on both sides.

9. Spoon about 2 tablespoons of the pea puree on each of 4 serving plates and top with a piece of tofu. Garnish with carrot relish and scallions or cilantro. Put a grit cake on each plate and serve.

RACHEL'S TIP

Wasabi isn't just a three-alarm wake-up call—it also packs anti-inflammatory, antibacterial, and potential anticancer properties.

Carrot Relish

CHUCK: *I make this carrot relish to accompany the tofu on page 91, but its uses are far more reaching. Serve it alongside any Asian-inspired dish, particularly sushi, or anytime you want something crunchy and bursting with flavor.* Makes about ¾ cup

½ cup rice vinegar

2 teaspoons salt

2 teaspoons sugar

¼ teaspoon dried red chili flakes

1 cup shredded carrot

2 teaspoons chopped cilantro leaves

1 teaspoon toasted sesame seeds, see Note

1 teaspoon canola oil, preferably expeller-pressed

½ teaspoon sesame oil

Note: To toast the sesame seeds, spread them in a small, dry skillet and toast over medium heat, stirring until they darken a shade and are fragrant, 40 to 60 seconds.

1. In a small saucepan, combine the vinegar, salt, sugar, and chili flakes with ½ cup of water. Bring to a boil over high heat.
2. Put the carrots in a small glass bowl and pour the boiling liquid over them to cover. Let the carrots soak for at least 1 hour but no longer than 2 hours.
3. Drain the pickling liquid from carrots and discard. Stir in the cilantro, sesame seeds, canola oil, and sesame oil, cover, and refrigerate for at least 2 hours before serving. The relish can be refrigerated for up to 3 days if well covered.

Quinoa-Stuffed Poblano Peppers with Salsa Romesco

CHUCK: *This vegan main course makes good use of quinoa, one of the most nutritious and most ancient of grains (although in fact it's a seed, not a grain, but who really minds?). Beyond this, both Sheryl and I like its nuttiness and light, fluffy texture, which seems custom-made to join with mild poblano peppers and smoky romesco sauce.* Serves 4

3 tablespoons canola oil, preferably expeller-pressed

1 medium-size onion, diced

1 large red bell pepper, seeded and diced

2 teaspoons chopped fresh garlic

1 tablespoon tomato paste

1 teaspoon ground cumin

1 teaspoon chili powder

¼ teaspoon dried red chili flakes

6 ounces Mexican or American beer

3 cups cooked quinoa, see Note on page 96

One 15-ounce can black beans, drained, preferably organic

1 bunch scallion, green parts only, trimmed and sliced

Grated zest of 1 lime

1 tablespoon chopped cilantro

4 poblano peppers, halved lengthwise and seeded

Kosher salt and freshly ground black pepper

8 ounces shredded soy cheddar or low-fat cheese

2 cups Romesco Sauce, page 97

Lime wedges, for garnish, optional

Chopped cilantro, for garnish, optional

Chopped scallions, for garnish, optional

1. In a medium-size saucepan, heat 2 tablespoons of the canola oil over medium-high heat and when hot, sauté the onions, bell pepper, and garlic for 3 to 4 minutes. Add the tomato paste, cumin, chili powder, and pepper flakes and cook until well blended, about 2 minutes longer. Pour the beer into the pan and cook, stirring, until nearly all the liquid evaporates.

2. Remove the pan from the heat and stir in the quinoa, beans, scallions, lime zest, and cilantro.

3. Preheat the oven to 350°F. Lightly spray a baking sheet with canola oil spray.

4. Put the poblano peppers, cavity side up, on the baking sheet and coat each lightly with the remaining tablespoon of canola oil (you may not need the entire tablespoon), and season with salt and pepper, to taste. Spoon about $1/2$ cup of the quinoa stuffing into each pepper. Top with the shredded cheese and bake until the cheese melts and the pepper is soft, 10 to 12 minutes.

5. Spoon $1/2$ cup of the romesco sauce on each of 4 serving plates and top with 2 stuffed pepper halves. Garnish each plate with a lime wedge, cilantro, and/or scallions.

QUESTIONS ABOUT QUINOA?

Every time I see anything written about quinoa, its pronunciation is always explained in the first sentence. I guess I should get that out of the way, too. It's "keen-wah." Quinoa is so hearty and adaptable it even grows high in the Peruvian Andes, where it has been a staple for centuries. Evidently the Incas recognized its nutritious properties and fed it to their warriors.

Like most plants, quinoa does better at slightly lower altitudes where the soil is apt to be richer and more aerated, but it's amazingly flexible. Quinoa is called an ancient grain, although actually it is a seed, and not a grain. I am just happy it is becoming increasingly popular in this country. Sheryl and I like the nutty flavor and the light, fluffy, slightly crunchy texture. And we both appreciate how healthful it is.

What makes it so good for you? Quinoa is high in protein, iron, and calcium and is a great source of all eight essential amino acids. It is a good source of lysine, which helps the body grow and repair tissue. Plus, it is rich in vitamins and minerals such as manganese, magnesium, iron, copper, and phosphorus. Best of all for vegans and others, quinoa is a complete protein.

When you cook quinoa, follow the instructions on the package. Remember that it needs to be soaked for about 15 minutes to loosen its outer coating, which can taste slightly bitter. Rinse the soaked quinoa thoroughly to wash away that coating, and finally cook the seed in a lot of water—about one and a half times as much as the amount of quinoa—and a little salt. For instance, if you want to cook 1 cup of quinoa, cook it in at least 1½ cups of water. If you want to cook 2 cups of quinoa, cook it in 3 cups of water. A cup requires about 15 minutes to cook, followed by 5 minutes or so to steam in the covered pot, very similarly to rice. Quick, easy, and so good for you.

Romesco Sauce

CHUCK: *Romesco sauce is one of the most adaptable in any cook's arsenal. Catalan in origin, the almond-and-bread based sauce made also from tomatoes and red bell peppers has been adopted by countries far from Spain because of its powerful yet mild flavor and pleasing texture. It tastes delicious with seafood—think crab cakes, grilled shrimp, and fish kebabs—and is also terrific as a warm dip for tortillas. Try it with the Mexican sandwiches called tortas, serve it with roasted and grilled vegetables, and even as a complement to leg of lamb. Thin the sauce with poultry or vegetable stock to convert it into a warm soup.* Makes about 2 cups

5 medium-size tomatoes, coarsely chopped

1 large red bell pepper, seeded and coarsely chopped

1 tablespoon chopped garlic

2 tablespoons canola oil, preferably expeller-pressed

1 cup torn stale bread pieces

½ cup toasted almonds

2½ tablespoons red wine vinegar

¼ teaspoon dried red chili flakes

Kosher salt and freshly ground black pepper

⅓ cup olive oil

1. Preheat the oven to 375°F. Lightly spray a baking sheet with canola oil spray.

2. In a large bowl, toss together the tomatoes, bell peppers, garlic, and canola oil. Spread the vegetables on the baking sheet and roast until the peppers begin to soften, 10 to 15 minutes. Watch carefully that the garlic does not burn.

3. In the bowl of a food processor fitted with the metal blade, process the roasted vegetable mixture with the bread, almonds, vinegar, and dried pepper flakes for 2 to 3 minutes or until fairly smooth but not completely pureed. Turn off the food processor and scrape down the sides. Season to taste with salt and pepper.

4. With the processor running, drizzle the olive oil through the feed tube as the sauce emulsifies. If the sauce is too thick, thin it with a little water, 1 teaspoon at a time.

Side Dishes

Grilled Asparagus and Red Peppers

CHUCK: *Everyone loves asparagus, which is at its best in the spring and early summer. This is a simple way to cook it—and believe me, once you try grilled asparagus you'll never go back to steaming. If you're worried about the spears falling through the grilling grate—and they might, which is annoying—enclose them in a grilling basket. When I'm on the road, I rarely set up an actual charcoal grill but cook the asparagus in a grill pan.* Serves 4

1½ pounds asparagus

1½ teaspoons extra-virgin olive oil

1 teaspoon garlic powder

Kosher salt and freshly ground black pepper

¼ cup sliced jarred roasted red peppers, preferably organic

Grated zest of ½ lemon

1. Prepare a gas or charcoal grill so that the heating elements or charcoal are medium-hot. Before you start the fire, rub the grate with a little canola oil to prevent sticking.
2. Break the asparagus stems where they naturally break off. Toss the trimmed asparagus in a mixing bowl and add the olive oil and garlic powder. Toss to coat and then season generously with salt and pepper.
3. Lay the asparagus on the grill and cook for 1 to 2 minutes. Using tongs, turn the asparagus over and then grill for about 1 minute longer or until the asparagus soften.
4. Return the asparagus to the bowl and add the peppers and lemon zest. Toss gently and serve.

HOW TO ROAST RED PEPPERS

Roasted red peppers from a jar work well in most recipes, and may be the easiest choice, particularly if you can't find organic peppers to roast—so you may as well make your life a little easier! Still, I usually roast my own peppers, primarily because I like the way they taste. You can roast them in a 400°F oven, under a hot broiler, on a grill, or over a gas flame. The trick is to let the peppers char fairly evenly on all sides. This takes 10 to 15 minutes in all, and you must turn the peppers several times during roasting to blacken the skin. If you choose to char them over a flame, hold the peppers with large, long-handled tongs or spear them with a long-handled fork.

Once the peppers are blackened, let them cool. Enclosing them in a paper or plastic bag works well, because the peppers steam as they cool, which helps to loosen the skin. When the peppers are cool enough to handle, it's an easy task to rub off the charred skin. If a little blackened char remains on the pepper, all the better; it looks authentic. Next, cut the peppers into pieces and scrape away and discard the seeds and membranes. The peppers are now ready to use.

Edamame Succotash

CHUCK: *In this succotash, the edamame stands in for the more expected lima beans—but actually, these plump, satisfying little beans shouldn't "stand in" for anything, but instead stand very much on their own. You may have only tried them in Asian restaurants as a salty pre-dinner snack, for they have long been a source of protein in Asia, but they are also making happy inroads here. The green soybeans have now become so popular, you can buy them already podded and par cooked in the frozen-food section of the supermarket.*

Edamame are picked when the soybeans are perfectly ripe, just before they begin to harden. I mix them with tomatoes, corn, peppers, and a little soy bacon for a succotash that tastes good with just about any fish or poultry dish. Even if you don't like tofu, I hope you'll try this. Edamame are soybeans but they don't taste anything like tofu; nor do they share its texture. Serves 4 to 6

2 teaspoons canola oil, preferably expeller-pressed
¼ cup diced red bell pepper
¼ cup diced red onion
2 teaspoons chopped garlic
1 cup roasted corn, see Cooking Corn on page 60
1 cup frozen shelled edamame
2 tablespoons cooked, chopped nitrate-free Smart Bacon or organic bacon
¼ cup dry white wine
¼ cup seeded and diced fresh Roma tomatoes, or another ripe tomato
1 tablespoon soy butter or unsalted butter
1 tablespoon chopped flat-leaf parsley
Kosher salt and freshly ground black pepper

1. In a large sauté pan, heat the canola oil over medium-high heat. When hot, sauté the bell pepper, onion, and garlic until softened, 3 to 4 minutes. Stir in the corn, edamame, and bacon and cook for 2 to 3 minutes longer.
2. Pour the wine into the pan and stir with a wooden spoon, scraping the bottom to loosen any sticking vegetables. Add the tomatoes and cook until warmed through. Add the butter and let it melt. Stir in the parsley, season to taste with salt and pepper, and serve right away.

Curried Cauliflower

SHERYL: *As I wrote earlier in the book, I consulted with the nutritionist Rachel Beller to help me tailor my post-cancer-treatment diet to boost my immune system. She taught me the value of cruciferous vegetables, members of the cabbage family, and consequently, I rediscovered cauliflower. When you think about it, how often do you actually eat it? Not often, I would bet! I didn't, either, but now it's a familiar part of my diet. Chuck has figured out some wonderful ways to serve it, such as this dish, which we like to call "cauliflower couscous" because of the final texture.* Serves 4 to 6

1 tablespoon canola oil, preferably
   expeller-pressed
½ cup shredded carrots
½ medium-size onion, diced
1 teaspoon chopped fresh ginger
1 teaspoon chopped garlic
1½ teaspoons mild yellow curry powder
½ teaspoon ground cumin
¼ teaspoon ground cinnamon

¼ cup vegetable broth
1 tablespoon freshly squeezed lemon
   juice
1 large head cauliflower, stem
   removed, grated
Salt and freshly ground black pepper
1 cup finely sliced fresh spinach leaves

1. In a large pot, heat the oil over medium-high heat until shimmering. When hot, sauté the carrots, onion, ginger, and garlic until they begin to soften, 2 to 3 minutes. Stir in the curry powder, cumin, and cinnamon.

2. Add the broth and lemon juice and cook, stirring gently to prevent the vegetables from sticking to the bottom of the pan. Add the grated cauliflower and season to taste with salt and pepper. Stir well to incorporate all ingredients.

3. Cover and let the cauliflower steam for 7 to 8 minutes, stirring once. The texture should resemble cooked couscous—tender but not mushy. Taste and adjust the salt and pepper.

4. Fold the spinach into the cauliflower and, using a slotted spoon, immediately serve the vegetables. Do not let the spinach cook for any length of time; it will soften and wilt sufficiently in the hot cauliflower.

Grilled Vegan Summer Squash Casserole

CHUCK: *If you're reading this recipe in July or August, you know all about bumper crops of yellow and green (zucchini) squash that hit the stores this time of year. What to do with it all? I decided to make a casserole, and while this one is a great side dish, it could also be a main course for a light summer meal. You could use regular mayonnaise instead of Vegenaise and dairy cheese instead of the soy cheese and turn this into a more ordinary vegetarian dish, rather than a vegan one.*

Serves 6 to 8

¼ pound yellow squash, cut into ⅛-inch-thick disks (about 3 cups)

¼ pound zucchini, cut into ⅛-inch-thick disks (about 3 cups)

1½ tablespoons canola oil, preferably expeller-pressed

1 teaspoon dried thyme

3 tablespoons soy butter

1 medium onion, sliced

2 cups sliced cremini or button mushrooms

2 teaspoons chopped garlic

1 tablespoon cornstarch

½ cup Vegenaise, see Note on page 178

Kosher salt and freshly ground black pepper

1 cup grated soy cheese

1¼ cups whole-wheat bread crumbs, lightly seasoned with kosher salt and freshly
  ground black pepper

1. Prepare a gas or charcoal grill so that the heating elements or charcoal are medium-hot. Before you start the fire, rub the grate with a little canola oil to prevent sticking.
2. In a mixing bowl, toss the yellow squash and zucchini with the canola oil and dried thyme.
3. Using long-handled tongs, grill each slice carefully for about 2 minutes on each side, until grill marks appear. Transfer the grilled squash to a baking sheet and let them cool to room temperature.

4. Meanwhile, in a medium-size skillet, heat the soy butter over medium heat and when melted, sauté the onion for 2 to 3 minutes. Add the mushrooms and garlic and cook, stirring, until softened, 3 to 4 minutes. Remove the pan from the heat and let the vegetables cool for 12 to 15 minutes.
5. Preheat the oven to 350°F.
6. In a large bowl, toss the grilled squash with the mushroom mixture.
7. In a small bowl, stir the cornstarch with 1 tablespoon of water to make a slurry.
8. Put the Vegenaise in a mixing bowl and whisk the slurry into it until thoroughly incorporated. Transfer to the vegetables and toss to mix evenly. Season to taste with salt and pepper.
9. Spread the mixture in a 9 x 9-inch baking pan, sprinkle with the cheese to cover evenly, and then scatter the bread crumbs over the casserole.
10. Bake for 20 to 25 minutes or until the casserole bubbles around the edges. Let the casserole cool for 5 to 10 minutes before serving.

Black Bean and Roasted Corn Sauté

CHUCK: *In this sauté, roasted corn mixed with the black beans really tastes good, but if you think it's too much of a bother to roast the corn for just a third of a cup, certainly feel free to use frozen organic corn kernels. Okay by me, but for the best flavor, buy an ear of corn and roast it in the oven as described on page 60. In the same vein, I know most people will use canned black beans, which are very good— particularly if you buy organic beans, which are sold in the natural foods section of most supermarkets. But if you have time, cook dried black beans that you have soaked for several hours. You need only a half cup here but you can cook up a big pot to eat in other ways all week long.* Serves 4

1 tablespoon canola oil, preferably expeller-pressed

¼ cup red onion, diced

2 teaspoons chopped garlic

½ cup cooked or canned black beans

⅓ cup roasted corn (1 medium-size ear), see Cooking Corn on page 60

⅓ cup diced seeded tomato

3 tablespoons diced pickled cactus, see Note

1 tablespoon chopped cilantro leaves

Kosher salt and freshly ground black pepper

Note: Pickled cactus is sold in glass jars in Mexican and Latin American markets or sections of supermarkets, where it might be called *Nopalitos escabeche.*

1. In a large sauté pan, heat oil over medium-high heat. When hot, cook the onion and garlic for 2 to 3 minutes. Add the black beans, corn, tomato, and cactus and continue to cook until everything is warmed through, about 2 minutes. Add the fresh cilantro and season with salt and pepper.

Sofrito Rice with Green Chiles and Mango

CHUCK: *I usually serve this rice with the Mojo Criollo Slow-Braised Pork (page 78) and suggest you do the same if you're looking for a side dish. It's also good with other pork or chicken dishes, particularly any with Latin flair. I like it with high-quality white rice, but if you are trying to eat only brown rice, don't let that stop you from trying this.* Serves 6 to 8

2 tablespoons canola oil, preferably expeller-pressed

1½ teaspoons annatto seeds

¼ cup coarsely chopped onion

¼ cup coarsely chopped, seeded poblano pepper

1 tablespoon chopped garlic

2 tablespoons chopped cilantro leaves

1 teaspoon dried oregano

½ teaspoon kosher salt

1 tablespoon tomato paste, preferably organic

1¾ cups vegetable stock, preferably organic

1 cup long or medium-grain rice

4 ounces canned green chiles, preferably organic, diced but not drained

1 cup diced fresh mango

¼ cup sliced scallions, white and green parts

Note: Annatto seeds are sold in Latin American markets and many specialty stores. You may also find them in many supermarkets and online.

1. In a small sauté pan, heat the canola oil and annatto seeds over medium heat and cook until the oil turns orangey-red, 3 to 5 minutes. Strain the oil through a fine-mesh sieve into a medium-size pot.

2. In the bowl of a food processor fitted with the metal blade, pulse the onion, poblano pepper, garlic, 1 tablespoon of the cilantro, oregano, and salt 4 to 5 times or until well mixed.

3. Heat annatto oil over medium-high heat and when hot, cook the processed vegetables until soft, 5 to 6 minutes. Stir in the tomato paste and cook for 2 to 3 minutes longer.

4. Add broth and whisk well while the liquid comes to a boil over medium-high heat. Add the rice, stir for 30 seconds, cover, reduce the heat to low, and simmer for about 20 minutes. Adjust the heat up or down to maintain the simmer. Remove the rice from the heat and let it sit, still covered, to steam for 2 to 3 minutes.

5. Stir in the green chiles, mango, scallions, and the remaining tablespoon of cilantro. Fluff gently with a fork until all ingredients are combined. Serve right away.

Corn and Thyme Pancakes

CHUCK: *I'll let you in on a secret: I have made similar pancakes from sugar-free pancake mixes, which I jazz up by adding roasted corn kernels, a few eggs, and herbs such as dried thyme. I do this for convenience when I'm cooking before a show: Since I travel with a big griddle, making these pancakes on the road is pretty easy (especially with a mix), but starting from scratch is always a little better.*

The pancakes add substance to any meal, and are a happy surprise. They aren't just for breakfast! I like to serve these as the base for a lightly dressed green salad, topped with a chicken breast or fish fillet. They are an integral part of the recipe for Free-Range Organic "Airliner" Chicken Breasts (page 76). Makes six 6-inch pancakes

½ cup unbleached all-purpose flour
½ cup stone-ground yellow cornmeal
1 teaspoon baking powder
1 teaspoon garlic powder
½ teaspoon kosher salt
¼ teaspoon freshly ground black pepper
2 large eggs, preferably omega-3 eggs
1 large egg yolk

½ cup milk
1 tablespoon canola oil, preferably
    expeller-pressed
¾ cup cooked corn kernels
½ bunch scallions, trimmed and sliced,
    white and green parts
1 tablespoon chopped fresh thyme
    leaves

1. In the bowl of a standing mixer fitted with the whisk attachment, whisk together the flour, cornmeal, baking powder, garlic powder, salt, and pepper until evenly blended. (Alternatively, you can whisk the batter together by hand.)
2. Add the eggs, egg yolk, milk, and canola oil and mix gently to form a batter.
3. Remove the bowl from the mixer and stir in the corn, scallions, and thyme.
4. Heat a large nonstick skillet over medium heat and when hot, ladle about 3 tablespoons of batter onto the pan and using the back of the ladle smooth the batter into a round cake. Cook for about 2 minutes, turn, and cook for about 2 minutes longer or until the pancake is nicely browned on both sides. Repeat with the remaining batter to make 6 pancakes.
5. If not using right away, wrap the pancakes in aluminum foil to keep warm.

Sesame-Shiitake Grit Cakes

SHERYL: *This is a shining example of Chuck's creativity. He's taken grits, a common staple in most Southern homes, and turned it into amazing-tasting cakes to serve as a side dish. I love these because they have no gluten and while I am not sensitive to it, I have cut back on it for health reasons. I particularly like my kids to avoid gluten, as it bogs down the immune system and contributes to chest colds. I also love shiitake mushrooms. They taste great and have healing benefits in their ability to fight infection and disease with the active compound they contain called lentinan. Chuck developed these sesame-flavored cakes to serve with the Asian-Marinated Tofu with Pea-Wasabi Coulis (page 91). Serves 4; makes eight or nine 2-inch cakes*

2 tablespoons canola oil, preferably expeller-pressed

2½ cups sliced shiitake mushrooms

¾ tablespoon finely chopped fresh, peeled ginger

½ tablespoon chopped garlic

6 cups vegetable broth

2 tablespoons soy sauce

1½ cups stone-ground grits, preferably organic

1 tablespoon soy butter or unsalted butter

1 tablespoon black sesame seeds

2 teaspoons sesame oil

2 teaspoons kosher salt

1 teaspoon freshly ground black pepper

½ bunch scallions, trimmed and sliced, white and green parts

1. Preheat the oven to 350°F.
2. In a medium saucepan, heat the canola oil over medium heat and when hot, sauté the mushrooms, ginger, and garlic for 3 to 4 minutes or until the mushrooms soften. Add the vegetable broth and soy sauce and bring to a gentle simmer. Reduce the heat to medium-low, and adjust it up or down to maintain the simmer.

3. With the mixture simmering, gradually whisk in the grits and cook, stirring, for 20 to 25 minutes. Add the butter, sesame seeds, sesame oil, salt, and pepper. When the butter is well incorporated, stir in the scallions.

4. With a spatula, scrape the grits into an 8 x 8-inch baking pan and smooth the top. Bake for 15 to 17 minutes or until the grits are fully set.

5. Let the grits cool for 30 minutes and then cut into squares. Serve immediately. (Alternatively, make the grits a day ahead, refrigerate, and warm slowly in a 200°F oven for 40 to 50 minutes before serving.)

RACHEL'S TIP

Mushrooms have it all: meaty flavor, protein, probiotics, antioxidants, selenium, B vitamins, fiber, iron, zinc, potassium, and properties that are anti-inflammatory, antibacterial, and antiviral. But wait, there's more: Mushrooms also boost immunity, lower blood pressure and cholesterol, detoxify the liver, and reduce the risk of cancer.

Desserts

Grilled Peaches and Cream

CHUCK: *When I travel with the band, coming up with dessert can be tough. Everyone likes something sweet after the meal, but before a performance no one wants it to be heavy or sugary. Summer fruit is one of the best choices. In fact, this dessert is the recipe that caught Sheryl's attention and pretty much launched the book! I suggest grilling peaches when they are ripe but still a little firm—not quite as soft as you might like them for eating out of hand. Just a short time on a grill (or in a grill pan) caramelizes the natural sugars in the fruit and also scores them with appealing grill marks. The lavender provides a delicate flavor that may be hard to place but is nonetheless irresistible. You can use full-, low-, or nonfat cream cheese or, for a vegan dessert, Tofutti cream cheese.* Serves 4

> 2 large, ripe peaches
>
> 2 tablespoons honey
>
> 2 teaspoons canola oil, preferably expeller-pressed
>
> 4 ounces cream cheese, softened
>
> 1 teaspoon freshly squeezed lemon juice
>
> 1 tablespoon dried lavender
>
> About 2 tablespoons chopped mint leaves or 8 whole mint leaves,
>
>   for garnish, optional

Note: For an intense mint flavor, stir the chopped mint leaves into the cream cheese filling. The mint and lavender are incredible together!

1. Prepare a gas or charcoal grill so that the heating elements or charcoal are medium-hot. Before you start the fire, rub the grate with a little canola oil to prevent sticking.

2. Cut the peaches in half and scoop out the pit to leave a cavity for the cream cheese. Cut a small slice off the rounded outside of the peach to allow it to sit flat on a plate.

3. Put the peaches in a large mixing bowl and gently toss with 1 tablespoon of the honey and the canola oil.

4. Put the peaches, cavity sides down, on the grill and cook for about 2 minutes. Turn the peaches over and continue to grill for about 1 minute longer or until

softened but not mushy. Remove the peaches from the grill and refrigerate until ready to serve. (Alternatively, grill the peaches following the same directions and using a grill pan set over the stove's burner.)

5. Meanwhile, in the bowl of a food processor fitted with the metal blade or in a bowl, process or whisk the cream cheese with the remaining tablespoon of honey, lemon juice, and lavender. Transfer the cream cheese to a zipped plastic bag and refrigerate for at least 1 hour and up to 24 hours.

6. When you are ready to serve, remove the peaches and cream cheese filling from the refrigerator and snip off a bottom corner from the plastic bag. Pipe the cream cheese filling into the peach cavities by squeezing it through the snipped corner of the bag. Serve immediately or refrigerate for up to 3 hours, garnishing with mint, if desired.

Blueberry "Pomegranita"

SHERYL: *Of all the desserts Chuck has created, this is among my favorites. So many studies have surfaced in recent years affirming the great health benefits of blueberries and pomegranates. Blueberries nearly always show up on the short list of "super foods" as they are packed with vitamins and minerals and, most impressive, are among the best antioxidants around. They are really low in calories, too, so this icy dessert is one I can indulge in without guilt!* Makes 4 to 5 servings

> 3 cups blueberry-pomegranate juice
>
> ½ cup sugar
>
> 2 teaspoons freshly squeezed lemon juice
>
> Pomegranate seeds, for garnish
>
> Fresh blueberries, for garnish

1. In a mixing bowl, stir together the blueberry-pomegranate juice, sugar, and lemon juice. Add 1 cup of water and stir until well mixed. Pour into a shallow metal or plastic pan and freeze for 2 hours.

2. After 2 hours, remove the pan from the freezer and stir the partially frozen granita with a fork. Return it to the freezer for 1 more hour. Remove and stir, breaking up the frozen, icy shards, and freeze again.

3. Repeat this freezing and stirring process every hour for 6 to 8 hours, or until the granita is completely frozen but not so solid it can't be scooped into bowls.

4. Serve the granita garnished with pomegranate seeds and blueberries.

RACHEL'S TIP

Pomegranate seeds contain high levels of breast-cancer-fighting ellagic acid. Want to maximize the benefits of this oil? Chew the seeds!

Chilled Melon Soup with Watermelon Salsa

CHUCK: *Because Sheryl never wants a heavy dessert before she goes on stage, this is always a good choice. The cool soup, made with summer cantaloupe and thickened with dense yogurt, needs only a little garnish of diced watermelon, kiwi, and mint leaves. Of course, the garnish is not absolutely necessary but it looks pretty and provides good texture against the smooth consistency of the melon soup.*

Serves 4 to 6

½ cup diced, seedless watermelon

1 kiwi, peeled and diced small

2 good-size mint leaves, chopped

1 medium-size ripe cantaloupe, peeled, seeded, and chopped (about 3 cups)

6 ounces plain soy yogurt, preferably organic

6 ounces peach or vanilla dairy or soy yogurt , preferably organic

½ cup freshly squeezed orange juice

1½ teaspoons agave nectar

¼ teaspoon kosher salt

1. In a small glass bowl, combine the watermelon, kiwi, and mint. Cover and refrigerate until ready to serve.
2. In a blender, blend half of the cantaloupe, half the yogurts, and ¼ cup of the orange juice on medium speed until very smooth. Transfer to a plastic or glass container. Repeat with the remaining half of these ingredients.
3. Whisk in the agave nectar and salt until all soup is well mixed. Cover and refrigerate for 1 to 2 hours. Serve garnished with the watermelon salsa.

Lemon-Vanilla Panna Cotta with Basil-Apricot Compote

CHUCK: *Panna cotta, particularly when made with soy milk and sweetened with agave nectar, is a light, mild-tasting pudding that slips down the throat without any heavy aftertaste. Pretty much a perfect dessert for a musician about to perform, I'd say. The compote adds texture, color, and interest to the panna cotta, which is an Italian phrase meaning "cooked cream." All through Italy panna cotta is considered about as basic and simple a dessert as there is.* Serves 4

Note: Agar agar powder is made from a type of red algae with significant gelling properties. I like to use it because it is not animal-based, and works so well. It's sold in natural food stores and some supermarkets.

PANNA COTTA

1 cup lemon soy yogurt

1 cup vanilla soy milk

2 teaspoons agave nectar

2 teaspoons agar agar powder, see Note

1 teaspoon pure vanilla extract

½ teaspoon finely grated lemon zest

BASIL-APRICOT COMPOTE

6 to 7 apricots, skin on, halved, pitted, and quartered (about 1½ cups)

2 tablespoons orange-flavored liqueur, such as Grand Marnier or Cointreau

2 tablespoons sugar

1 teaspoon pure vanilla extract

1½ tablespoons chopped fresh basil leaves

1. To make the panna cotta: In medium saucepan, combine the yogurt, milk, nectar, agar agar powder, vanilla, and lemon zest and cook, whisking often, on medium heat until well blended and the lemon oil is extracted from the zest, 6 to 7 minutes. Remove from heat and let the mixture cool slightly.

2. Lightly spray four 8-ounce ramekins with canola oil cooking spray. Pour the panna cotta into each ramekin and refrigerate, uncovered, until chilled, at least 2 hours. Cover the chilled ramekins and refrigerate until ready to serve.

3. To make the compote: In a medium-size saucepan, combine the apricots, liqueur, sugar, vanilla, and ¹/₂ cup of water and bring to a boil over medium-high heat.

Reduce the heat to medium and cook until the compote looks amalgamated, 10 to 12 minutes.

4. Remove the pan from the heat and transfer the compote into a glass container. Refrigerate for 30 minutes. At this point, stir in the basil and refrigerate for at least 2 hours longer, and up to 8 hours. For longer storage, cover well and refrigerate for up to 3 days. The basil will turn brown during storage, so try to use it before that happens.

5. To serve, gently run a knife around the outside edge of each ramekin. Invert a serving plate on top of each one and, holding the plate and ramekin, flip them so that the panna cotta slides out onto the plate. Serve garnished with 2 to 3 tablespoons of the compote.

AGAVE NECTAR EXPLAINED

Agave nectar, sometimes called agave syrup, is the sweetener of choice for many cooks, including me, in part because its glycemic index is lower than that of table sugar or even honey—and because a little goes a long way. It's nice when you don't want to use very much sweetener at all. It tastes similar to honey but is a little milder. It's less viscous, too.

Most agave nectar is made from blue agave plants, which grow primarily in southern Mexico. There are many varieties of agave plants (tequila is distilled from agave) but blue agave is the plant used most often for nectar. When the extracted sap is processed into nectar, it's heated at a low temperature to break carbohydrates into sugar. (The low temperature allows raw food enthusiasts to embrace agave nectar; it's not really "cooked.")

I like agave nectar for any number of reasons, not the least being that it dissolves quickly in cold liquids. It's great for the melon soup on page 121, for example, and can also be used to sweeten cold drinks.

Vegan Chocolate-Mint Brownies

SHERYL: *I like to make Chuck's vegan brownies at home for Wyatt. I love the fact that they are more healthful than regular brownies and that the hint of mint adds an interesting, fresh taste that both Wyatt and I love. Plus, Wyatt loves licking the spatula!* Makes about 15 brownies

2 cups unbleached all-purpose flour

2 cups raw sugar, preferably organic

½ cup unsweetened cocoa powder

1 teaspoon baking powder

1 teaspoon iodized salt

1 cup vegetable or canola oil

1 to 1½ teaspoons peppermint extract

1 teaspoon pure vanilla extract

½ cup carob chips

1. Preheat the oven to 350°F degrees. Grease a 13 x 9-inch baking pan.
2. In the bowl of an electric mixer fitted with the paddle attachment and set on low speed, mix together the flour, sugar, cocoa powder, baking powder, and salt.
3. Once the dry ingredients are mixed together, turn off the motor and add the oil, 1 cup of water, 1 teaspoon of peppermint extract, and the vanilla extract. With the mixer on medium-high, beat the batter so that it is well incorporated and smooth. Taste and add more peppermint extract, if desired. Stir in the carob chips by hand.
4. Pour the batter into the prepared pan and smooth the surface with a rubber spatula. Bake for 25 to 30 minutes or until a toothpick inserted in the center comes out clean.
5. Let the brownies cool in the pan set on a wire rack for 10 to 15 minutes. Cut into squares to serve.

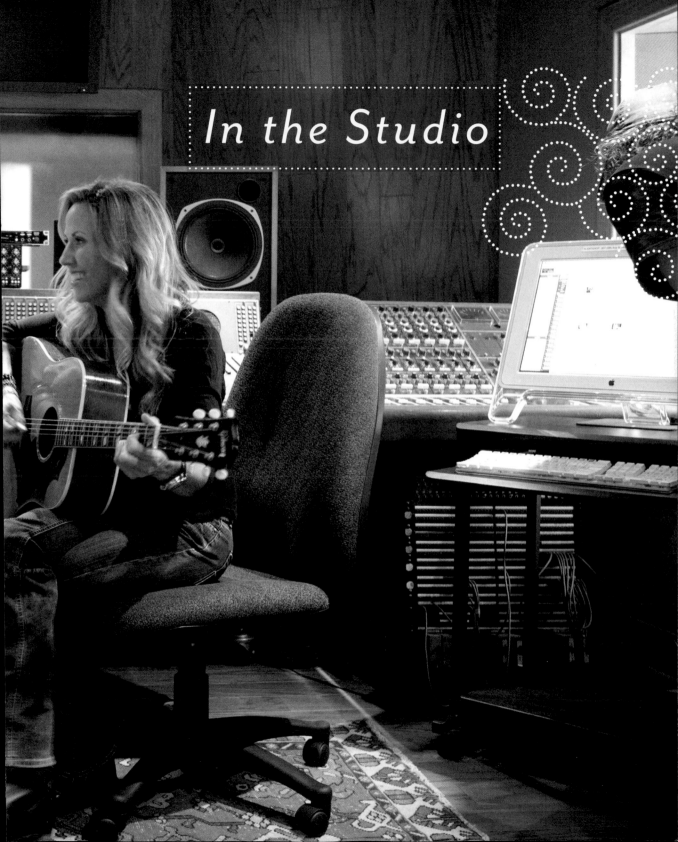

In the Studio

Fall and Winter

Wyatt was three months old when I started recording the Detours record in 2007. I had completed radiation and changed the way I approached my diet by the time he entered my life. It was a wonderful time at my Nashville farm, as the two of us were surrounded by friends and loved ones throughout the entire recording process. Wyatt was passed around from person to person as each of us recorded our parts. He was truly a studio baby.

Our days consisted of working during the day, taking a break for Chuck's healthy snacks around 4:00 P.M., and sitting down to a delicious 7:30 P.M. dinner, complete with good wine and great conversation. Every evening, we had a chosen topic of conversation or game, whether it be the "three truths and a lie" game or "your list of overrated" or simply a subject of interest. And every memorable dining experience there at the farm was accentuated by a beautiful menu Chuck created. Even his presentation was inspired. What a huge difference it made not to have to halt the recording process to think about

what we would order in from which Nashville restaurant. Good food and great fellowship and inspired music-making were the ingredients for a perfect recording experience.

Fall and winter tend to be the months I record, with spring and summer being about touring. Just as he does when we are touring, Chuck prepares super-healthy, balanced meals that rely on seasonal and organic produce. The food is pure, clean, simple, and always amazing and creative. It's harder to eat locally in the cold weather. There is not much growing in Tennessee during January and February, but Chuck manages to work with whatever is available.

This is when a more Eskimo-like diet kicks into gear very nicely. I call it that because it includes a lot of salmon and colorful vegetables, such as butternut squash, sweet potatoes, broccoli, cabbage, and Brussels sprouts, all easily secured during the winter, along with brown rice. When I started eating this way, right after I was diagnosed with breast cancer in 2006, I almost OD'd on salmon, but Chuck figured out so many ways to prepare it and other good-for-you fish that I am totally happy. These days, I eat fish at least three times a week and love every bite. I also know I am eating for my health with the assurance that my breast cancer will have to fight me to come back!

Appetizers and Snacks

Smoky White Bean and Rosemary Spread

CHUCK: *The secret to this spread—or you could call it a dip—is the smoked paprika. It's a fairly powerful spice, and so I advise you to use a little less than I have suggested and taste before adding more of it. I always have the paprika on hand. It's sold in Middle Eastern markets and gourmet shops and of course you can order it online. I like to serve it on crostini or pita chips. I also like it on bruschetta with an arugula salad. You won't get the same result with liquid smoke, but it could be used instead.* Makes about 2 cups

2 cups cooked or canned cannellini beans, drained

2 tablespoons freshly squeezed lemon juice

1½ teaspoons finely chopped rosemary leaves

1½ teaspoons smoked paprika or liquid smoke

1 teaspoon coarsely chopped garlic

¼ cup olive oil

Kosher salt and freshly ground black pepper

1. In the bowl of a food processor fitted with the metal blade, process the beans, lemon juice, rosemary, paprika, and garlic until smooth, 2 to 3 minutes. Scrape down the sides of the bowl.

2. With the motor running, drizzle the olive oil through the feed tube until the spread is smooth. Season to taste with salt and pepper and pulse once or twice to mix. Use immediately or refrigerate for up to 2 weeks in a lidded container.

Sweet and Spicy Edamame

CHUCK: *I talk about edamame on page 102 with the recipe for Edamame Succotash, explaining exactly what it is and why it is so good for you. The buttery green soybeans are great as a side dish, but they also make a perfect appetizer or snack. I prepare these so that they are sweet (from the honey), spicy (from the sriracha sauce), and salty all at once. These flavors wake up the palate and distinguish this dish from more traditional "sushi house" edamame.* Serves 2 to 3

2 teaspoons kosher salt

One 1-pound bag frozen edamame

1 tablespoon light soy sauce

1½ teaspoons honey

1 teaspoon sesame oil

½ teaspoon sriracha sauce or another hot chili sauce

1 teaspoon sea salt

1 teaspoon sesame seeds, toasted, see Note on page 93

1. In a medium-size pot or large saucepan, bring 2 quarts of water and the kosher salt to a boil over medium-high heat. Add the edamame, stir once or twice, and when the water returns to a boil, reduce the heat and simmer briskly for 4 to 5 minutes if frozen or 2 to 3 minutes if thawed, or until the edamame are bright green. Using a slotted spoon, transfer the edamame to a serving bowl.

2. Add the soy sauce, honey, sesame oil, sriracha sauce, sea salt, and sesame seeds and toss gently. Serve while still warm.

Jack Daniel's–Glazed Pork Tenderloin and Sweet Potato Skewers

SHERYL: *Little skewers of tender pork and sweet potatoes are one of my favorite appetizers, as Chuck knows. I could make a meal of them—and sometimes have done so—they are so good. And the sweet potatoes, which pair perfectly with the pork, fit into my desire to eat a wide range of colorful vegetables. They are just better for you, and I am all for that!* Serves 5 to 6; makes fifteen to eighteen 6-inch skewers

GLAZE

1 cup Jack Daniel's or another Tennessee-style whiskey

1 teaspoon light soy sauce

1 tablespoon cornstarch

Kosher salt and freshly ground black pepper

SKEWERS

1 medium-size organic pork tenderloin (about 1¼ pounds), cut into ¾-inch cubes

2 tablespoons store-bought blackening seasoning, such as Zatarain's, Chef Paul's, or Cabela's Open Season blends, see Note

1 teaspoon smoked paprika, optional

2 tablespoons canola oil, preferably expeller-pressed

2 large sweet potatoes, peeled and cut into ½-inch cubes

15 to 20 bamboo skewers, about 6 inches long

Note: Check the salt content of these blends. Some may be salt-free, so you can adjust the salt to your taste.

1. To make the glaze: In a small saucepan, bring the Jack Daniel's, 4 tablespoons of water, and soy sauce to a boil and cook, whisking once or twice, for 2 to 3 minutes. Reduce the heat so that the liquid simmers gently.

2. Meanwhile, in a small bowl, whisk together the cornstarch and 1 tablespoon of water. Add this to the pan and slowly whisk into the glaze until slightly thickened. Season to taste with salt and pepper.

3. Transfer the glaze to a glass container, cover, and refrigerate for at least 2 hours and up to 8 hours.

4. To prepare the pork skewers: In a glass, ceramic, or other nonreactive mixing bowl toss the pork with half the blackening seasoning, half the paprika, and half the oil until evenly coated. Cover and refrigerate for at least 2 hours and up to 8 hours. (Alternatively, marinate the pork in a gallon-size, sealable plastic bag.)

5. In a separate glass, ceramic, or other nonreactive mixing bowl, toss the sweet potatoes with the remaining blackening seasoning, paprika, and oil. Cover and refrigerate to marinate for at least 2 hours and up to 8 hours. (Alternatively, marinate the potatoes in a gallon-size, sealable plastic bag.)

6. Preheat the oven to 425°F. Line 2 medium-size roasting pans with aluminum foil and lightly oil the foil.

7. Arrange the pork in one pan and the potatoes in the other. Spread the food out so that it will cook evenly. Brush the pork with a quarter of the glaze and the potatoes with a quarter. Set aside the remaining half of the glaze. (To avoid cross-contamination, pour the desired amount of glaze into a small bowl and use a brush designated for the pork to brush the glaze over the meat.)

8. Cook both the pork and sweet potatoes for 15 to 18 minutes or until the pork is cooked through and the potatoes are fork tender. If either is not done after 18 minutes, return the pan to the oven for about 5 minutes longer.

9. Meanwhile, in a small dish, soak the bamboo skewers in cool tap water to cover for about 20 minutes. This prevents the skewers from scorching when they are on the grill.

10. Remove the pans from the oven and set aside so that the pork and potatoes can cool to room temperature.

11. Thread a piece of potato and a piece of pork on each skewer and return the skewers to one of the roasting pans. Brush with the remaining glaze and serve right away or hold in a 200°F oven to keep them warm for up to 35 minutes. (Alternatively, for tailgating, grill the assembled skewers for 2 to 3 minutes to reheat them.)

Phyllo-Wrapped and Pistachio Shrimp with Sweet Chili Sauce

CHUCK: *When Sheryl throws a dinner party, these are a great favorite. They take some time to make, especially depending on how many you need, but the reward is well worth it. Crispy, flaky phyllo dresses up so many dishes and is so easy to use, you might cast about for ways to use it over and over, as I did. The sweet chili sauce, which you can find in the Asian food section of the market, pairs wonderfully with the shrimp. I can't deny these have a lot of fat, and both Sheryl and I consider them "special occasion" treats. They are so rich, you don't have to eat more than one or two to feel pampered and indulged.* Serves 8 to 10; makes 24

8 sheets frozen phyllo dough, see Note

12 tablespoons (1½ sticks) margarine or soy butter, melted
  (I like to use Smart Balance margarine)

¾ cup shelled pistachios, finely chopped

24 jumbo shrimp, peeled and deveined, with tail on

Kosher salt and freshly ground black pepper

Sweet chili sauce (bottled)

Note: Phyllo is sold frozen in supermarkets and comes in 1-pound packages, usually holding 20 sheets.

1. Remove the phyllo from the freezer, unwrap it, and leave it out for 15 to 20 minutes to come to room temperature. Once the phyllo reaches room temperature, cover it with a damp paper towel to keep it moist.

2. Preheat the oven to 350°F. Line a baking sheet with aluminum foil and lightly oil the foil.

3. Lay 1 sheet of phyllo on a work surface so that it is horizontal. Brush it evenly with melted margarine and then lay a second sheet of phyllo over the first and brush with more margarine. Cover the phyllo sheets completely with the margarine but do not drench them.

4. With a sharp knife, cut vertically down the sheet to make 6 strips, each about 1½ inches wide. Without moving the strips, dust the phyllo with pistachios.

5. Season the shrimp well with salt and pepper and then put 1 on the bottom of a

strip of phyllo. Roll a shrimp in the phyllo strip, beginning at the bottom of the strip and rolling to the top. The tail will extend from one end of the dough roll. Continue to roll shrimp in the remaining strips and as each is rolled, transfer it to the baking sheet, arranging the rolls so that they do not touch.

6. Repeat with more phyllo, margarine, pistachio crumbs, and shrimp until all the shrimp are rolled in phyllo. (At this point, the shrimp can be cooked or covered with plastic wrap and refrigerated for up to 2 hours.)

7. Bake the shrimp until the phyllo is golden brown, about 20 minutes.

8. Let the shrimp cool for about 5 minutes on the baking sheet and then serve with the chili sauce for dipping.

Vegan Reuben

CHUCK: *When I switched to a mainly vegetarian diet, I missed Reuben sandwiches. Who knew corned beef would rank so high with my taste memory? Because it did, I immediately set about creating an acceptable alternative. Corned Beef Seitan, which I explain how to make on page 142, came to the rescue with flying colors and absolutely no sacrifice of flavor. You can buy it at natural food stores if you don't want to take the extra time to make it. And for meat eaters? This sandwich is fantastic made with the "real thing."* Serves 6

> 12 slices rye or pumpernickel bread
> 6 tablespoons Vegan Thousand Island Dressing, page 178
> 1½ pounds Corned Beef Seitan (page 142), or store-bought seitan (24 to 30 slices)
> 1½ cups Quick Red Cabbage Sauerkraut, page 229
> 6 to 12 slices vegan Swiss or soy cheese
> 6 tablespoons soy butter or unsalted butter

1. Assemble 6 sandwiches by constructing each one in this order: 1 slice bread, 1 tablespoon dressing, 4 or 5 slices of seitan, about ¼ cup sauerkraut, and 1 to 2 slices cheese. Finally, put another slice of bread on top of the sandwich.
2. Heat a good-size skillet over medium heat and when hot, melt 1 tablespoon of the butter. Put the sandwich in pan and cook on each side for 2 to 3 minutes or until golden brown and the cheese is melted. Repeat with the remaining ingredients to make 6 sandwiches.
3. Cut each sandwich in half and serve.

Corned Beef Seitan

CHUCK: *Corned seitan shares a meaty flavor and texture with corned beef, and as a wheat product, is a great source of protein, without the fat and cholesterol. You can use this for sandwiches or as a topper for crackers. To make it, you will need cheesecloth and a few lengths of butcher's twine or other string, so don't be caught short-handed.* Makes about 1½ pounds

Note: Vital wheat gluten is sold in natural food stores and some large supermarkets in sacks, much like flour. It's often used to help the texture of yeast breads. The gluten contains approximately 75 percent protein, and as such is an important component for a balanced diet.

2 cups vital wheat gluten, see Note

3 tablespoons ground pickling spice for meat (I use Morton & Basset brand)

2 tablespoons onion powder

1 tablespoon smoked paprika

1 tablespoon garlic powder

1 tablespoon salt

1 cup vegetable broth

½ cup canola oil, preferably expeller-pressed

1½ tablespoons light soy sauce

1½ tablespoons real maple syrup

1 tablespoon apple cider vinegar

12 ounces dark or stout beer

1 cup chopped celery

1 cup chopped carrot

1 cup chopped onion

2 bay leaves

1. In a large mixing bowl, whisk together the wheat gluten, pickling spice, onion powder, paprika, garlic powder, and salt.

2. In another bowl, whisk together the broth, oil, soy sauce, syrup, and vinegar. Pour the mixture into the mixing bowl with the dry ingredients and stir until the dough is well blended.

3. Using damp hands, shape the dough into a loaf about 1½ inches thick. Wrap in a double layer of cheesecloth, twist the ends closed, and tie with butcher's twine.

4. Meanwhile, in a medium saucepan, combine about 1 gallon of water with the beer, celery, carrots, onion, and bay leaves and bring to a simmer over medium heat.

5. Lower the loaf into the simmering liquid and cook for about 1 hour and 15 minutes, turning the loaf occasionally. Adjust the heat up or down to maintain the simmer.

6. Remove the seitan from the simmering liquid and let it rest for about 15 minutes. Unwrap the seitan and transfer to a plate. Refrigerate for at least 45 minutes before slicing.

Hot Mulled Apple Cider

SHERYL: *Hot apple cider is one of autumn's true joys. Wyatt is a fan, too, but of course he only gets the G-rated version. If you can find a local apple orchard that presses its own cider, buy it. If it's organic, all the better. If not, look for natural and organic cider in the markets.* Serves 6 to 8

½ gallon (8 cups) fresh, unfiltered apple cider, preferably organic
Grated zest of 1 orange
10 whole cloves
4 cinnamon sticks
½ cup Jack Daniel's or another Tennessee-style whiskey, optional
¼ cup packed light brown sugar
½ teaspoon freshly ground nutmeg

1. In a medium-size pot, bring the cider to a simmer over medium-high heat. When it simmers, add the orange zest, cloves, cinnamon sticks, whiskey (if using), brown sugar, and nutmeg. Stir well.
2. Let the cider return to a simmer and cook for about 20 minutes, adjusting the heat up or down to maintain the simmer.
3. Strain through a fine-mesh sieve or chinois and serve warm.

Cross Creek Cream

SHERYL: *Every December, our farm manager Chuck Coorts, a.k.a. Chuck #1 (no relation to Chuck White!), makes this decadent, creamy holiday cocktail. This is definitely not "healthy," but something everyone appreciates during the holidays. We wrap it up and label it for our friends and neighbors. It's sort of a chocolately eggnog and is named for Cross Creek Farm, where Wyatt, Levi, and I live, outside Nashville. We try to use local and organic ingredients from nearby surrounding farms. Don't use more than the half teaspoon of almond extract to avoid overpowering the drink, and keep the mixture refrigerated (this is super important because of the raw eggs). This is made to sip on during the festivities of the season, so take it easy, and enjoy.* Serves 6

2½ cups bourbon (we use Evan Williams, best bourbon for the money!)

One 14-ounce can sweetened condensed milk

1 cup local heavy cream

3 large organic eggs, preferably omega-3 eggs, lightly beaten

2½ tablespoons organic chocolate syrup (Santa Cruz brand or you could substitute Hersheys)

2 teaspoons pure vanilla extract

½ teaspoon almond extract

1. In a blender, mix together the bourbon, condensed milk, and cream. Add the beaten eggs and blend until well mixed. Add the chocolate syrup, vanilla, and almond extract and blend for about 1 minute.
2. Pour the mixture into a large pitcher, cover and chill for at least 1 hour and up to 2 days. When thoroughly chilled, pour into small glasses and serve. (Or like we do it on the farm, after it is well blended, pour the drink into pint mason jars, chill, and pass around to all your friends to drink right out of the jars!)

Soups

Blackened Butternut Squash Soup, Nutmeg
Crème Fraîche, and Fried Leeks   150

Vegan Black-Eyed Pea Soup with Sweet
Green Chili Cornbread Muffins   154

Warm Hummus Soup with Cilantro Pesto
and Garlicky Pita Chips   157

Hot-and-Sour Miso Soup with Tofu and Baby Bok Choy   160

Blackened Butternut Squash Soup, Nutmeg Crème Fraîche, and Fried Leeks

SHERYL: *I love this soup. I have always loved orange-hued butternut squash, so it was easy to work it into meals as part of my "colorful veggies" requirement. Chuck makes this with low-fat milk instead of cream, and then enriches it with a dollop of crème fraîche. He says he roasts the squash to deepen its flavor and I have to believe him. This soup rocks!* Serves 4 to 6

FRIED LEEKS

3 cups canola oil, preferably expeller-pressed

1 cup thinly sliced leeks, dark green tops removed, washed thoroughly (1 large leek)

1 teaspoon kosher salt

NUTMEG CRÈME FRAÎCHE

1 cup Crème Fraîche, page 153, or store-bought crème fraîche

1 to 1½ teaspoons ground nutmeg (freshly ground if possible)

Kosher salt and freshly ground black pepper

SOUP

1 large butternut squash, peeled, seeded, and cut into ½-inch cubes

2½ tablespoons canola oil, preferably expeller-pressed

1 tablespoon plus 1 teaspoon store-bought low-sodium blackening seasoning, such as Zatarain's, Chef Paul's, or Cabela's Open Season blends

1 medium yellow onion, julienned

1 tablespoon chopped garlic

6 cups low-fat milk or unsweetened soy milk

2 bay leaves

Kosher salt and freshly ground black pepper

2 teaspoons freshly squeezed lemon juice

Micro greens for garnish (optional)

1. To make the fried leeks: In a heavy, medium-size pot or large saucepan, heat the oil over medium-high heat to a temperature of 325°F, as registered on a deep-fat

fryer thermometer or candy thermometer. Line a plate with several layers of paper towels and set it close to the stove.

2. Drop half of the leeks into the hot oil and stir them with long-handled tongs. Let them fry to 2 to 3 minutes or until the white slices are lightly golden and the light green slices are brighter green. They will be done when they stop sizzling. Using the tongs, lift the leeks from the oil and drain on paper towels. Lightly salt the leeks while they are warm.

3. Allow the oil to regain its temperature and repeat the frying with the remaining leeks. When all the leeks have been fried, set them aside at room temperature until needed and for up to 3 hours.

4. To make the crème fraîche: In a small bowl, whisk together the crème fraîche and 1 teaspoon of nutmeg. Taste and add more nutmeg and season with salt and pepper. Transfer to a plastic squirt bottle or plastic container with a tight-fitting lid and refrigerate until needed, for up to 3 days.

5. To make the soup: Preheat the oven to 400°F. Line a shallow baking pan, approximately 13 x 9 inches, with aluminum foil or lightly oil it with canola oil spray.

6. Put the diced squash in a large bowl and toss with 1¹/₂ tablespoons of the oil and the blackening seasoning. *Do not add salt at this time.* Spread the squash on the baking pan and roast for 20 to 25 minutes or until the squash is soft and cooked through.

7. In a medium pot large enough to hold the squash easily, heat the remaining 1 tablespoon of canola oil over medium-high heat and when hot, sauté the onion for 2 to 3 minutes. After the first minute of sautéing, add the garlic and cook for the remaining 1 to 2 minutes, taking care the garlic does not burn. Add the milk and bay leaves and bring to a medium simmer. Do not boil. Cook for about 10 minutes, adjusting the heat up or down to maintain the simmer. Remove the bay leaves, add the roasted squash, and continue to simmer for 15 to 20 minutes.

8. Remove the pot from the heat and let the mixture cool slightly. Transfer half of the squash and milk to a blender and puree until smooth. Season to taste with salt and pepper while blending. Pour the soup into a clean pot. Puree and season the remaining mixture.

9. Bring the soup to a simmer over medium-high heat. Add the lemon juice and taste for seasoning.

10. When hot, ladle the soup into soup bowls and drizzle the crème fraîche in a circular pattern over the soup. Garnish each serving with a handful of fried leeks and a few sprigs of micro greens.

Chuck's Crème Fraîche

CHUCK: *It is easy to make homemade crème fraiche, and once you do it once or twice you will fall in love with its slightly tart creaminess. I like this dolloped on just about any soup, not only the butternut squash soup on page 150, and also drizzled over smoked salmon. It dresses up fresh berries, sliced peaches, and other fruit for dessert.* Makes about 1 cup

> 1 cup heavy cream
> 1 tablespoon buttermilk

1. In a glass bowl, stir the cream with the buttermilk. Cover the bowl with plastic wrap and let it sit at room temperature for 18 to 24 hours, or until thickened.

2. Use the crème fraiche right away or refrigerate, well covered, for up to 2 weeks. Stir before using.

Variation: Fast Crème Fraîche

Stir $\frac{1}{2}$ cup of whole-milk sour cream into the heavy cream and use right away. It will keep, covered and refrigerated, for up to 10 days.

Vegan Black-Eyed Pea Soup with Sweet Green Chili Cornbread Muffins

CHUCK: *I grew up eating black-eyed pea soup on New Year's Day, which is common in the South. The peas themselves represent coins and thus prosperity, and the more you eat, the more prosperous you will be and the better your luck in the coming year. I don't know if this is actually the case, but I happily chow down on this soup every January 1.* Serves 8 to 10

1½ pounds dried black-eyed peas

1 tablespoon canola oil, preferably expeller-pressed

1 large red onion, diced

¾ cup diced green bell pepper

3 to 4 slices bacon or Smart Bacon, cooked until nearly crisp and chopped (about ¾ cup)

2 quarts vegetable broth, preferably organic

1 bay leaf

Two 14- to 15-ounce cans diced tomatoes, preferably organic (do not drain)

Kosher salt and freshly ground black pepper

1 recipe Sweet Green Chili Corn Muffins, page 155

Vegan or dairy sour cream, for garnish, optional

Chow chow relish, for garnish, optional

1. Soak the black-eyed peas in about a quart of cold water to cover for 8 to 10 hours or overnight.
2. In a large pot, heat the canola oil over medium heat and when hot, sauté the onions and bell peppers until they begin to soften, 2 to 3 minutes. Add the bacon and continue to cook for another 2 minutes, stirring frequently. Add the vegetable broth and bay leaf and bring to a boil over high heat.
3. Add black-eyed peas to the boiling liquid, reduce the heat to medium, and simmer briskly for 1½ to 1¾ hours or until the beans are tender. Adjust the heat up or down to maintain a good simmer without letting the liquid boil.
4. Add the diced tomatoes and salt and pepper to taste, stir to mix, and remove

from the heat. If soup is too thick, add a little more vegetable stock or water.

5. To serve, ladle the hot soup into large, shallow soup bowls and crumble 1 muffin over each bowl.

Sweet Green Chili Corn Muffins

CHUCK: *Corn muffins, fresh from the oven, are incredibly tempting and fill the kitchen with warm, homey aromas. Surely anyone can come up with dozens of excuses to bake them—including me. I especially like them sliced in half and smothered with southern barbecue. I also crumble them for a nice cornbread salad. If you want plain muffins, leave out the green chiles.* Makes 12 muffins

> 1½ cups unbleached all-purpose flour
>
> 1½ cups stone-ground white or yellow cornmeal
>
> 2½ teaspoons baking powder
>
> 2 teaspoons garlic powder
>
> 2 teaspoons kosher salt
>
> 2 teaspoons freshly ground black pepper
>
> 1 teaspoon cumin
>
> One 4-ounce can diced green chiles, preferably organic
>
> 1¾ cups plain unsweetened soy milk or dairy milk
>
> 3 tablespoons canola oil, preferably expeller-pressed, or melted soy butter
>
> 2½ tablespoons honey

1. Preheat the oven to 400°F and grease a standard-size, 12-cup muffin pan.
2. In the bowl of an electric mixer and using a wire whisk, whisk together the flour, cornmeal, baking powder, garlic powder, salt, pepper, and cumin. Insert the paddle attachment and with the mixer on medium-high speed, beat in the green chiles, milk, oil, and honey until the batter is well mixed, 2 to 3 minutes.
3. Spoon the batter into the muffin pan so that each cup is three quarters full. Bake for 23 to 25 minutes or until lightly browned and a toothpick inserted in the center of a muffin comes out clean. Let the muffins cool in the pan set on a wire rack for about 10 minutes. Turn out onto the rack to cool completely.

Warm Hummus Soup with Cilantro Pesto and Garlicky Pita Chips

CHUCK: *I've gotten great reviews for this soup, which is essentially warm, thinned hummus garnished with pita chips and pesto. On a stormy winter day, it's warm and comforting and so hits the spot. Keep a few cans of chickpeas in the pantry and you can make this just about anytime. If you prefer, garnish the soup with smoked paprika and thick, plain yogurt instead of the pesto.* Serves 6 to 8

6 cups organic vegetable stock

Three 14- to 15-ounce cans organic chickpeas, drained and rinsed

4 tablespoons freshly squeezed lemon juice

3 tablespoons tahini paste

3 teaspoons chopped garlic

2 teaspoons ground cumin

2 teaspoons ground coriander

2 teaspoons turmeric

Kosher salt and freshly ground black pepper

12 to 24 Garlicky Pita Chips, page 158

6 to 8 tablespoons Cilantro Pesto, page 159

1. In a blender, blend half the stock, half the chickpeas, half of the lemon juice, half of the tahini paste, half of the garlic, and half of the cumin, coriander, and turmeric until smooth, 2 to 3 minutes. If the soup seems too thick, add water or more vegetable stock, 1 tablespoon at a time. Season to taste with salt and pepper. Transfer the first batch of the soup to a large saucepan or pot.
2. Repeat with the remaining half of those ingredients to blend a second batch.
3. When all the soup is blended and in the pot, bring it to a simmer over medium-low heat. Stir the soup occasionally during heating.
4. Ladle the soup into shallow bowls and top each serving with 2 or 3 pita chips. Spoon about 1 tablespoon of the pesto on the chips or soup.

Garlicky Pita Chips

CHUCK: *I suggest these with the hummus soup on page 157, and of course they would be excellent with plain hummus. They are nice for snacking and also can be crumbled over a salad. It's tempting to skip these and rely on store-bought pita chips, but I urge you to try them at least once to taste the difference.*

Makes 36 chips

3 whole-wheat pita rounds, cut into 6 segments (like a pizza)

1½ tablespoons olive oil

2 teaspoons garlic powder

2 teaspoons sea salt

1 teaspoon freshly ground black pepper

1. Preheat the oven to 350°F. Lightly oil 2 large baking sheets.
2. Separate the top of each pita from the bottom, so that each is divided into 2 halves. Transfer the halves to a large mixing bowl and sprinkle with the olive oil, garlic powder, salt, and pepper. Toss well but gently so that each pita triangle is well coated.
3. Lay the pita triangles on the baking sheets in a single layer. Bake for 10 to 12 minutes or until golden brown.
4. Let the pita chips cool on the baking sheets to room temperature. Use immediately or store in a sealed plastic bag or large lidded container for up to 1 week.

Cilantro Pesto

CHUCK: *Like any pesto, this is wonderful served with pasta, grilled meats, and thick, grilled fish steaks. I like it as a dip for pita chips and also spread on Cuban sandwiches and quesadillas.* Makes about 1½ cups

2 bunches cilantro, thick stems removed (2 to 3 loosely packed cups)
½ cup sliced, toasted almonds
1 small jalapeño, seeded and diced
1 tablespoon freshly squeezed lemon juice
1½ teaspoons chopped garlic
½ teaspoon kosher salt
¼ to ⅓ cup extra-virgin olive oil

1. In the bowl of a food proocessor fitted with the metal blade, process the cilantro, almonds, jalapeño, lemon juice, garlic, and salt until almost smooth.
2. With the processor running, slowly drizzle half of the olive oil into the pesto through the feed tube.
3. When half of the olive oil is incorporated, scrape down the sides of the food processor. Again, with the motor running, add the remaining oil, or enough to form a smooth, thick pesto.
4. Using a rubber spatula, scoop the pesto into a container with a tight-fitting lid. Use immediately or refrigerate for up to 3 days. The pesto is best eaten close to making.

Hot-and-Sour Miso Soup with Tofu and Baby Bok Choy

SHERYL: *I have come to love miso soup. The flavor is familiar to anyone who frequents Japanese restaurants, but as that was not my experience, I was much older when I acquired a taste for it. Who knew fermented soybeans could taste so good! And when Chuck makes miso soup, it tastes great. Most of all, I love the fact that it bursts with healthful properties. Some studies contend that a daily bowl of miso soup cuts the risk of breast cancer (Japanese women evidently eat miso just about every day and breast cancer is far less prevalent in Japan than here). I don't claim to be an expert on this, but I am happy to down this tasty miso soup whenever Chuck makes it. Miso is rich with antioxidants, and full of vitamins such as E, B12, and B3. These nutrients help strengthen the immune system, which I especially appreciate; with two young kids, I really can't afford to get a cold that might drain me of my much needed energy.* Serves 6 to 8

Note: Sheets of nori seaweed are sold in most natural food stores and some supermarkets. The thin, brittle, black sheets are 8 or 9 inches long and are very easy to work with.

1½ sheets nori paper seaweed, chopped or shredded roughly, see Note

1½ tablespoons rice wine vinegar

1½ tablespoons light soy sauce

½ teaspoon sriracha sauce or another red chili sauce, plus more if desired

¾ cup miso paste

1-pound block extra-firm tofu, cut into ¼- to ½-inch cubes

2 cups chopped baby bok choy leaves

1½ cups bean sprouts

1 bunch scallions, trimmed and sliced, white and green parts (7 or 8 scallions)

1 tablespoon chopped fresh cilantro

1. In a large pot, bring 8 cups of water, the nori, vinegar, soy sauce, and sriracha sauce to a simmer over medium-high heat. Cook for 5 to 6 minutes, adjusting the heat up or down to maintain the simmer.

2. Reduce the heat to low and stir in the miso paste. Whisk gently until dissolved and simmer for 1 to 2 minutes. Miso tends to "hang out" at the bottom of the pot, so be sure to stir deep into the broth to incorporate the miso.

3. Stir in the tofu, bok choy leaves, bean sprouts, scallions, and cilantro and simmer for 1 to 2 minutes longer. Remove from the heat and stir gently before serving. Be sure to scoop the tofu from the bottom of the pot when serving.

RACHEL'S TIP

Not all soy products are created equal. Forget soy isolates, concentrates, pills, and powders. Instead, seek out whole traditional soy foods, such as tempeh and tofu, which contain many cancer-protective substances.

Salads

Mixed Lettuces with Anjou Pears, Toasted Walnuts, Blue Cheese, and Pickled Red Onions

SHERYL: *Chuck knows how to put a salad together. He uses ingredients I would never think of but they always work beautifully. This is one of my favorites: The combination of pears and blue cheese is so yummy, and I especially love the nuts in this salad—nuts are among my favorite snack foods because a small handful goes a long way. Equally important, walnuts are a great source of fiber, B vitamins, vitamin E, and other antioxidants.* Serves 4

> 6 cups baby lettuces or mixed greens
>
> ½ cup Champagne Vinaigrette, page 177
>
> 2 Anjou pears, sliced and cored (not peeled)
>
> 1 cup toasted, roughly chopped walnuts, see Note
>
> ¾ cup crumbled blue cheese (3 to 4 ounces; I like Point Reyes or Humboldt Fog)
>
> ½ cup Pickled Red Onions, page 221

1. In a large mixing bowl, lightly toss the greens with ¼ cup of the vinaigrette. Divide the greens among 4 plates.
2. Lay 5 or 6 slices of pear on top of the greens on each plate. Top with a handful of walnuts, some crumbled blue cheese, and some pickled red onion. Drizzle the remaining vinaigrette over each salad and serve.

Note: To toast the walnuts, spread them in a dry skillet and heat them over medium heat, shaking the pan occasionally, for 6 to 8 minutes or until the nuts darken a few shades and are fragrant. Alternatively, you can roast walnuts in a 400°F oven, spread on a baking sheet, for 6 to 8 minutes.

RACHEL'S TIP

Walnuts come loaded with omega-3s, vitamins, minerals, protein, and fiber. And we're just getting started here. They also boost brain power, reduce stress, prevent heart disease, and help fight some cancers. What more could you want?

Haricots Verts Salad

SHERYL: *Pole beans, or string beans, were among the many fresh vegetables my mom and dad grew in their shared neighborhood garden co-op. How wonderful to be brought up with the "from the earth to the table" mentality, no matter how small the garden. I am trying to raise my boys with the same experience, and this salad is a delicious way to use fresh string beans straight from the garden.* Serves 4

Note: To toast the almonds, spread them in a dry skillet and heat them over medium heat for 4 to 6 minutes or until the nuts darken a few shades. Or roast them in a 400°F oven, spread on a baking sheet, for 4 to 6 minutes.

Kosher salt

2 cups trimmed haricots verts or other slender green beans

2 tablespoons sliced almonds, toasted, see Note

10 to 12 grape tomatoes, halved

¼ purple onion, thinly sliced

Juice of ½ lemon

1 tablespoon extra-virgin olive oil

Freshly ground black pepper

1. Put a bowl filled with cold water and ice cubes next to the sink.
2. Fill a large saucepan with water, salt it lightly, and bring to a boil over high heat. Add the beans and let the water return to the boil. Cook for 2 to 3 minutes or until slightly softened. Drain the beans and then submerge the beans in the ice water for 3 to 4 minutes. Drain again.
3. Lay the beans on paper towels or clean kitchen towels and pat them dry.
4. In a medium-size bowl, toss the beans with the almonds, tomatoes, onion, lemon juice, and olive oil. Season with salt and pepper and toss gently. Serve immediately.

RACHEL'S TIP

A squeeze of lemon juice makes salads even healthier, since the vitamin C enhances the absorption of nutrients from greens.

Baby Spinach Salad with White Balsamic–Tarragon Dressing

SHERYL: *Spinach is one of those outstanding foods that is exceedingly rich in antioxidants, as well as vitamins and minerals—particularly iron—and it also tastes great. It's a welcome change from a more expected mixed green type of salad. This salad seems typically autumnal to me—bolstered with grapes, toasted hazelnuts, and rich, buttery Brie cheese.* Serves 4

Note: To toast the hazelnuts, spread them in a single layer on a baking sheet and toast in a preheated 350°F oven for 10 to 15 minutes or until they deepen in color and the skins blister. Transfer the nuts to a clean, dry kitchen towel and rub them gently to remove the skins.

4 cups baby spinach leaves

3 tablespoons White Balsamic–Tarragon Dressing, page 179

One 4-ounce wedge Brie cheese, cut into 12 to 16 slices

¾ cup halved red or white seedless grapes

½ cup chopped, toasted hazelnuts, see Note

2 to 3 radishes, thinly sliced

1 tablespoon hazelnut oil

1. In a mixing bowl, toss the spinach with the dressing. Divide the salad among 4 serving plates.
2. Top each salad with Brie, grapes, hazelnuts, and sliced radish. Drizzle each salad with hazelnut oil and serve.

Roasted Beet Salad

CHUCK: *Not everyone is a fan of beets, which is a shame because when they are properly cooked, they are just amazing! Unfortunately, many of us think only of pickled beets when we consider the root vegetable, which don't hold a candle to roasted fresh beets, sliced and sprinkled with a light dressing. I begin with several different colors of fresh beets, preferably with the greens still attached, which reassures me that they were not picked months ago. I roast them in their skins for the best sweet, earthy flavor imaginable and rub off the skins after they are cooked. Pairing the root vegetables with oranges, orange juice, olive oil, and arugula challenges their intense flavor and will have you coming back for more—which is a good thing as beets are a great source of iron and antioxidants.* Serves 4

CANDIED PECANS

2 large egg whites, lightly beaten

1½ teaspoons sugar

1 teaspoon salt

½ teaspoon ground cinnamon

¼ teaspoon cayenne pepper

1 cup whole pecans

BEETS

2 medium red beets

2 medium golden beets

2 teaspoons canola oil, preferably expeller-pressed

Kosher salt and freshly ground black pepper

2 thick-skinned oranges (preferably not juice oranges)

⅓ cup extra-virgin olive oil

1 cup loosely packed arugula

½ red onion, thinly sliced

4 ounces fresh goat cheese

1. To make the candied pecans: Preheat the oven to 350°F. Line a well-oiled baking sheet with aluminum foil.

2. In a small bowl, whisk the egg whites with the sugar, salt, cinnamon, and cayenne pepper. Add the pecans and toss to coat. Lift the pecans from the whites with tongs or a slotted spoon and gently shake to let any excess egg whites slide back into the bowl. Spread the pecans on the prepared baking sheet.

3. Bake for about 5 minutes and then gently break up the pecans with a large spoon or spatula. Bake for 3 to 4 minutes longer or until the pecans are slightly darkened and crispy.

4. Transfer the pecans to a plate or dish to cool and break them into pieces. (If you don't use all the pecans, you can keep the rest for about a week in a tightly lidded container; they make a great snack.)

5. To prepare the beets: Preheat the oven to 375°F.

6. Trim the tops and bottoms of the beets and wash them under running water, scrubbing the skins well with a vegetable brush. Pat dry with paper towels or a kitchen towel.

7. Put the beets in a baking dish large enough to hold them in a single layer and toss with the canola oil and salt and pepper to taste. Cover the dish with aluminum foil and make a tight seal.

8. Bake for 45 to 50 minutes or until fork tender. Remove the beets from the pan and refrigerate for at least 15 minutes to cool them down. (They don't have to be cold.)

9. Meanwhile, peel the oranges with your fingers or a paring knife, being careful to remove as much of the white pith from the fruit as possible. Holding an orange over a bowl to catch the juices, separate the sections and let them drop into the bowl. You should have approximately 10 sections.

10. Squeeze the remaining orange and strain the juice. Put the orange segments in one container and the orange juice in another, adding any accumulated juice from the bowl holding the segments. Slowly whisk the olive oil into the juice until emulsified, season to taste with salt and pepper, cover, and refrigerate until ready to use.

11. Remove the beets from the refrigerator and, wearing rubber gloves, slowly remove the skin from the beets by gently rubbing each one with a paper towel. Slice the beets into rounds and return them to the refrigerator for another 20 minutes.

12. Put a small amount of arugula on one side of each plate. Shingle 4 to 5 slices of beets on top of the arugula, alternating the colors. Season to taste with salt and pepper. Top the beets on each plate with 2 or 3 orange segments, 7 to 8 slivers of red onion, $^1/_4$ cup of crumbled candied pecans, and 1 ounce crumbled goat cheese.

13. Whisk the orange dressing and drizzle a small amount over each salad and serve immediately.

Cyclops Salad

CHUCK: *I call this salad "cyclops" because the fried egg sitting on top resembles a single eye staring up at you. Until you take your fork to the yolk. When you do, the lovely yellow liquid adds a sauce-like consistency to the salad.* Serves 4

> 4 thin slices Italian bread (cut them from a large loaf, not a skinny one)
>
> About 3 tablespoons olive oil
>
> Kosher salt and freshly ground black pepper
>
> About 1 teaspoon garlic powder
>
> 3 cups half-stemmed watercress (trim the bottom halves
>   of the stems from the watercress before measuring; they tend to be bitter)
>
> ½ cup cooked or canned and drained cannellini or fava beans
>
> ¼ cup sliced roasted red peppers, preferably organic
>
> 1½ teaspoons truffle oil
>
> 2 lemons, halved
>
> 2 tablespoons soy or unsalted butter
>
> 4 large eggs, preferably omega-3 eggs
>
> One 3- to 4-ounce block Pecorino Romano
>   or Parmigiano-Reggiano cheese

1. Preheat the oven to 375°F. Line a baking sheet with aluminum foil.
2. In a medium bowl, toss the bread slices with 1 or 2 tablespoons of oil, salt, pepper, and garlic powder to taste. Lay the bread slices on the baking sheet and toast for 8 to 10 minutes. Turn them once during toasting to ensure even browning. Let the bread slices cool.
3. Put 1 slice of bread on each of 4 serving plates. Top each with an equal amount of watercress, beans, and peppers.
4. In a small bowl, whisk together the remaining 1 tablespoon of olive oil and the truffle oil, and season to taste with salt and pepper. Drizzle a small amount over each salad. Squeeze a lemon half over each salad.
5. When salad is complete, heat a medium-size skillet over medium heat and

when hot, melt the butter. Fry the eggs in the pan, turning them once to make eggs over easy. Season lightly with salt and pepper and then transfer an egg to the top of each salad.

6. Shave 5 to 6 slivers of cheese over each salad and serve.

RACHEL'S TIP

According to research, watercress has a plant compound that may reduce the risk of developing breast cancer.

Wheat Berry and Apple Salad with Cider Vinegar Dressing

CHUCK: *Although I came up with this wheat berry salad based on foods I could easily find in the supermarket in the fall and winter—apples, grapes, and walnuts—once I tossed and tasted the salad I realized it was similar to a Waldorf salad, minus the lettuce. The texture of the salad is an explosive amalgamation of chewy, crunchy, and tender; the flavors burst with nuttiness, tang, and sweetness. No wonder this is a great favorite with Sheryl and many others who gather at her Nashville studio during these cold months. Plus consider the mind-boggling health benefits of wheat berries, which include fiber, folic acid, protein, B vitamins, vitamins E and C, and minerals.* Serves 6 to 8

3 cups vegetable broth or water

1 cup uncooked wheat berries

1½ tablespoons apple cider vinegar

Grated zest of 1 lemon

4 to 5 tablespoons extra virgin olive oil

Kosher salt and freshly ground black pepper

⅔ cup diced tart apples, such as Granny Smith

⅔ cup halved red grapes

½ cup chopped toasted walnuts

¼ cup finely diced red onion

¼ cup finely diced celery

1 tablespoon chopped fresh basil leaves

1. In a medium-size saucepan, bring the vegetable broth (or water) to a boil over medium-high heat. Add the wheat berries, reduce the heat so that the liquid simmers, and cook until tender, about 45 minutes. Adjust the heat up or down to maintain the simmer. Drain the wheat berries through a colander and then spread the berries on a baking sheet to cool to room temperature, 30 to 45 minutes. You can refrigerate the wheat berries to speed the cooling process.

2. In a small bowl, whisk together the vinegar and lemon zest. Slowly add the oil, whisking constantly, until the dressing is emulsified. Season to taste with salt and pepper.

3. Transfer the cooled berries to a large mixing bowl. Add the apples, grapes, walnuts, onion, celery, and basil. Toss well to mix. Pour the whisked dressing over the salad and fold until the salad is evenly mixed and dressed.

4. Serve immediately or let the salad marinate for an hour or so. The salad can be covered and refrigerated for up to 4 days.

Champagne Vinaigrette

CHUCK: *In a classic vinaigrette, the ratio of vinegar to oil is 1:3, and this is no exception. I have added Dijon mustard to boost the flavor depth and help emulsify the dressing. I use this with the Mixed Lettuces with Anjou Pears, Toasted Walnuts, Blue Cheese, and Pickled Red Onions (page 165), and it would be outstanding with any leafy greens. If the salad includes fruit or berries, perfect!* Makes about 1 cup

> 2 tablespoons champagne vinegar
>
> 1 small shallot, finely chopped
>
> 2 teaspoons Dijon mustard
>
> 2 teaspoons honey
>
> 1 teaspoon garlic powder
>
> ¾ cup vegetable or canola oil
>
> Kosher salt and freshly ground black pepper

1. In a blender, blend the vinegar with the shallot, mustard, honey, and garlic powder just until mixed. With the blender on medium speed, slowly drizzle the oil through the feed tube and blend until the vinaigrette is emulsified. If the vinaigrette seems too thick, add water, 1 teaspoon at a time, until it reaches the desired consistency.

2. Season the vinaigrette with salt and pepper to taste. Use immediately or refrigerate. This will keep, well covered, in the refrigerator for up to 2 weeks. Shake or whisk well before using.

Vegan Thousand Island Dressing

CHUCK: *While I slather this on the Vegan Reuben sandwich (page 141), you will find this perfect for a salad or another sandwich that calls for Thousand Island dressing. It's vegan, but if you prefer egg-based mayo instead of the Vegenaise, go for it!* Makes about 1½ cups

Note: Vegenaise is egg-free mayonnaise. It's made by Follow Your Heart and is sold in natural food stores, some supermarkets, and gourmet shops. There are other brands, but I like this one the best.

1 cup Vegenaise, see Note
½ cup sweet pickle relish
¼ cup ketchup
½ teaspoon Worcestershire sauce
½ teaspoon freshly squeezed lemon juice
3 to 4 dashes hot pepper sauce, such as Tabasco
Kosher salt and freshly ground black pepper

1. In a medium bowl, whisk together the Vegenaise, relish, ketchup, Worcestershire sauce, lemon juice, and Tabasco. Season to taste with salt and pepper.
2. Use immediately or store in a lidded container for up to 2 weeks.

White Balsamic–Tarragon Dressing

CHUCK: *You can buy tarragon-infused vinegar, but I prefer to add fresh tarragon to the dressing and rely on unadulterated white balsamic vinegar. This is a terrific all-around dressing for anyone who likes the flavor of tarragon. I use it with the baby spinach salad on page 168.* Makes about 1 cup

2 tablespoons white balsamic vinegar

1 tablespoon chopped fresh tarragon

1 tablespoon diced red onion

2 teaspoons honey

1½ teaspoons Dijon mustard

½ teaspoon chopped garlic

¾ cup canola oil, preferably expeller-pressed

Kosher salt and freshly ground black pepper

1. In a blender, combine the vinegar, tarragon, onion, honey, mustard, and garlic. Blend on medium speed and with the motor running, slowly drizzle the oil through the feed tube. Blend until emulsified. Season to taste with salt and pepper. If the dressing is too thick, add water, 1 tablespoon at a time.
2. Put the lid on the blender canister and refrigerate for at least 1 hour before using. If not using right away, transfer to a lidded container and refrigerate for up to 2 weeks. Whisk well before using.

Main Courses

Grilled Grass-Fed Beef Tenderloin with Chanterelles, Leeks, and Purple Potatoes

CHUCK: *When I cook beef, I try very hard to make sure it's grass-fed. Sheryl and I both appreciate the humane way these cattle are raised: Grass-fed herds spend their entire lives living in open pastures where they can roam as the grass and the spirit will them. The cattle are slaughtered at slightly older ages than corn-fed beasts— without the corn diet, they take longer to reach optimum weight—and because they are not fed grain, the meat is leaner and tastes a little different from the heavily marbled beef most of us are accustomed to. But despite the difference, grass-fed beef is equally delicious! Farmers who raise grass-fed beef tend to participate in the sustainability and organic movements and so don't give the cattle growth hormones or unnecessary antibiotics.*

This dish, made with tenderloin, is an all-in-one meal, complete with potatoes and mushrooms. Tenderloin is also called filet mignon. To make this, you might choose to buy the whole tenderloin and cut your own portions. The soft, tender meat is easy to slice into round medallions. Serves 4

⅔ cup diced purple potatoes (½-inch dice) or another colorful potato variety

Four 6-ounce portions organic grass-fed beef tenderloins

Kosher salt and freshly ground black pepper

2 tablespoons canola oil, preferably expeller-pressed,
    plus 1½ tablespoons for sautéing vegetables

½ cup diced leeks, white parts only (about ½ large leek)

1 pound chanterelle mushrooms, cleaned and sliced

2 teaspoons chopped garlic

¼ cup brandy or cognac

1 tablespoon heavy cream

1 tablespoon soy butter or unsalted butter

½ tablespoon chopped flat-leaf parsley

1 teaspoon freshly squeezed lemon juice

About 1 cup micro greens, such as radishes, mesclun, red mustard,
    arugula, mâche, or pea shoots

1. Fill a large saucepan with lightly salted water and bring to a boil over high heat. Meanwhile, fill a bowl with ice and water and set it next to the stove. Cook the diced potatoes in the boiling water until softened, 10 to 12 minutes. Drain and immediately dunk the potatoes in the ice water to stop the cooking. Drain again and let the potatoes dry completely on paper towels.

2. Prepare a gas or charcoal grill so that the heating elements or charcoal are medium-hot. Before you start the fire, rub the grate with a little canola oil to prevent sticking.

3. Season each fillet with salt and pepper and lightly rub each with about $1/2$ tablespoon of canola oil.

4. Grill the tenderloins for 2 to 3 minutes on each side for medium rare or 3 to 4 minutes on each side for medium to medium well done. Transfer to a cutting board and let the meat rest for at least 5 minutes.

5. Meantime, in a medium-size sauté pan, heat the remaining $1 1/2$ tablespoons of canola oil over medium-high heat until slightly softened, 2 to 3 minutes. Add the leeks, mushrooms, and garlic and sauté for 2 to 3 minutes longer.

6. Add the potatoes and cook just until warmed. Add brandy and bring to a boil. Cook for about 2 to 3 minutes or until reduced by half. Stir in the cream, soy butter, parsley, and lemon juice. Season to taste with salt and pepper.

7. To serve, spoon equal amounts of the mushroom mixture onto the center of each of 4 serving plates. Top each with a fillet and garnish with micro greens.

RACHEL'S TIP

Grass-fed beef contains less saturated fat and 60 percent more omega-3s than grain-fed beef.

Five-Spiced Pork Tenderloin with Sautéed Fig and Plum Sauce

SHERYL: *I grew up eating a lot of pork . . . "the other white meat," as we called it. Pork seems a natural in cold weather, and so when Chuck made this with its seductive fig and plum sauce, I was blown away. (He says peaches or apples work, too.) Pork pairs so naturally with the fruity sauce—what a great combination of flavors. We feel strongly about only eating meat that has been responsibly raised and so avoid pork from large farms and instead buy heritage breeds raised by local farmers near my place outside Nashville.* Serves 4 to 6

> 2 whole pork tenderloins, trimmed of any fat or sinew (each about 1¼ pounds), preferably heritage pork, see The Right Pork on page 189
>
> 2 tablespoons Five-Spice Powder, homemade (page 190) or store-bought
>
> 2 teaspoons of kosher salt, plus more to taste
>
> 2 tablespoons canola oil, preferably expeller-pressed
>
> ½ sweet onion, thinly sliced
>
> 4 to 5 fresh figs, stemmed and quartered (about ¾ cup)
>
> 3 to 4 fresh plums, pitted and cut into ¼-inch-thick slices (about ¾ cup)
>
> 1 cup light red wine, such as Sangiovese or Beaujolais nouveau
>
> 1 tablespoon sugar
>
> 1 tablespoon soy butter or unsalted butter
>
> ½ tablespoon chopped fresh tarragon leaves
>
> Freshly ground black pepper

1. Lay the tenderloins in a large glass baking dish and sprinkle with the five-spice powder and 2 teaspoons of salt. Rub 1 tablespoon of the oil into the meat, making sure the tenderloins are evenly covered. Cover the dish with plastic and refrigerate for at least 1 hour and up to 6 hours.

2. Heat a large sauté pan over medium-high heat and heat the remaining table-spoon of oil. When the oil is hot, sauté the onion for 3 to 4 minutes. Add the figs and plums and toss gently. Stir in the red wine and sugar and bring the wine to a boil. Cook until reduced by half, 1 to 2 minutes. Remove the pan from

the heat and stir in the butter and tarragon, stirring to melt the butter. Season to taste with salt and pepper. Cover and set aside.

3. Prepare a gas or charcoal grill so that the heating elements or charcoal are medium-hot. Before you start the fire, rub the grate with a little canola oil to prevent sticking.

4. Lift the tenderloins from the glass dish and grill for 2 to 3 minutes on each side, turning the tenderloins with long-handled tongs until nicely browned. Cover the grill and cook the meat for a total of 10 to 12 minutes for medium-done meat and 15 to 17 minutes for medium-well meat. Transfer the tenderloins to a cutting board and let them rest for about 10 minutes. (Alternatively, sear the

THE RIGHT PORK

Sheryl and I both support humane and responsible animal husbandry, which is why when I cook pork for her, I am careful about where the meat comes from. Around Nashville this is pretty easy to do because I have discovered markets and farmers who sell locally raised heritage breeds. Otherwise, I can order the meat from reliable Internet sites.

This specialty pork tastes much better than anything you can buy in large supermarkets. It's full of rich flavor, most likely similar to that of the hogs butchered on nearly every small American farm in the nineteenth and early twentieth centuries. Because these heritage breeds do not thrive on large, industrial operations, it's up to the small farmer to keep them from extinction. Most were imported to this country from Europe hundreds of years ago and include Berkshire, Gloucestershire Old Spot, Large Black, Tamworth, and Yorkshire pigs. Butchers who sell them stock pure- or cross-bred meat. Many have been bred with Asian hog breeds with great results.

If your local farmers' market or gourmet store stocks heritage pork, try it. It's worth the extra cost—maybe you won't eat pork as often but when you do, you will enjoy it more.

Finally, some folks still believe pork has to be "cooked to death" to make it okay to eat. This is not true with today's meat, which is safe and only needs to be cooked until its internal temperature reaches 155° to 160°F. Additionally, pork is lower in fat and cholesterol than it once was, which makes it a healthful alternative to other meats.

tenderloins in a lightly oiled nonstick skillet over medium-high heat for 2 to 3 minutes on each side until nicely browned. Transfer the pork to a lightly oiled roasting pan and cook in a 425°F oven for about 15 minutes for medium done and 17 to 20 minutes for medium-well done.)

5. Slice the pork into slices about ¼ to ½ inch thick. To serve, shingle 3 to 4 slices of pork on 4 to 6 plates and spoon the pan sauce over the meat.

Five-Spice Powder

CHUCK: *This spice mixture enhances the pork tenderloins on page 187, but I bet you never thought of sprinkling a little over the apples for a pie. Try it! It's also great with stir-frys and will improve the flavor of many storebought barbecue sauces.* Makes about ⅔ cup

2 tablespoons ground cinnamon

2 tablespoons ground dried wild ginger or other ground ginger, optional

2 tablespoons ground star anise

2 tablespoons fennel seeds

2 tablespoons whole cloves

¼ teaspoon black peppercorns

1. Put all the ingredients into a spice or coffee grinder and process into a powder. Transfer the powder to a container with a tight-fitting lid. The powder will keep in a cool, dark place for up to 6 months.

RACHEL'S TIP

The "cinnamon" you find in stores is really cassia. True cinnamon, known as Ceylon cinnamon, is worth the time it takes to find as well as the slight extra cost since it contains greater health benefits. Look for Ceylon cinnamon in spice shops, specialty stores, and online.

Pomegranate and Rosemary–Marinated Lamb Loin

SHERYL: *Chuck knows I was not a fan of lamb before he changed my mind with this dish. The root vegetables are just right with the meat, and I particularly appreciate that Chuck marinates the lamb in super-healthful pomegranate juice. I drink far more pomegranate juice these days than I ever imagined I would, even mixing it with my beloved Diet Sprite (at Chuck's suggestion). Pomegranates are little powerhouses, packed with vitamins C and B5 as well as antioxidants that get rid of harmful free radicals in the body. There's ongoing research investigating properties in the fruit that might lower blood pressure, prevent heart disease, and even inhibit the growth of breast cancer cells.* Serves 4

MARINATED LAMB

2 cups pomegranate juice

3 shallots, sliced thinly (¼ to ⅓ cup)

¼ cup olive oil

1 tablespoon chopped garlic

1 tablespoon chopped fresh rosemary

Kosher salt and freshly ground black pepper

4 to 5 sprigs fresh thyme

4 to 5 sprigs fresh mint

2 whole racks of lamb, with loins removed from bones, see Note

SAUCE

2 cups low-sodium organic beef broth

1 cup dry red wine

8 to 10 whole black peppercorns

2 cloves garlic, peeled and lightly smashed with the side of a chef's knife

3 to 4 sprigs fresh mint

3 sprigs fresh thyme

1 sprig fresh rosemary

1 bay leaf

Kosher salt and freshly ground black pepper

Note: You can cut the meaty part of the loin chops from the rack or ask the butcher to do it for you. All you are doing is removing the meat from the bones. Discard the bones or save them to make stock.

Kosher salt and freshly ground black pepper

3 tablespoons Dijon mustard

1 cup panko bread crumbs, seasoned with a little salt and pepper

1 recipe Roasted Root Vegetables, page 220

1. To marinate the lamb: In a glass, ceramic, or other nonreactive bowl, combine the pomegranate juice, shallots, oil, garlic, rosemary, 2 teaspoons of salt, and 2 teaspoons of pepper and whisk thoroughly until well mixed. Drop the thyme and mint sprigs into the marinade.

2. Put the lamb in another glass, ceramic, or other nonreactive dish large enough to hold the meat, or in a large, sealable plastic bag. Pour the marinade over the lamb and turn to coat or push around in the sealed bag.

3. Refrigerate for at least 4 hours and for no longer than 24 hours, turning the loins periodically to make sure they are well coated with marinade. If using a plastic bag, turn the bag several times during marinating.

4. Meanwhile, make the sauce. In a medium-size saucepan, bring the broth and wine to a boil. Reduce the heat to medium and simmer for 2 to 3 minutes to blend the flavors and reduce the liquids slightly. Add the peppercorns, garlic, mint, thyme, rosemary, and bay leaf and simmer gently, adjusting the heat to maintain the simmer, until the sauce reduces by half, 20 to 25 minutes. Taste and adjust the seasoning with salt and pepper. Cover and set aside to keep warm until needed.

5. To cook the lamb: Preheat the oven to 375°F and prepare a gas or charcoal grill so that the heating elements or charcoal are medium-hot. Before you start the fire, rub the grate with a little canola oil to prevent sticking. (Alternatively, heat a large countertop grill or use a grill pan or large skillet set over medium-high heat.)

6. Remove the lamb from the marinade and pat off any excess ingredients with paper towels. Season the meat with salt and pepper and rub with a little canola oil. Sear the lamb on the grill, or in the hot pan, on all 4 sides, about 1 minute per side, until the meat is lightly charred. Set the lamb aside off the heat for about 5 minutes to cool slightly.

7. Meanwhile, preheat the oven to 375°F. Take a roasting pan large enough to hold the lamb easily and line it with aluminum foil. Spread a little oil over the foil.

8. When cool enough to handle, rub the mustard liberally over the charred lamb.

9. Spread the bread crumbs in a shallow dish. Lay the lamb in the crumbs and turn it in the crumbs until well coated.

10. Transfer the lamb to the roasting pan and cook for 8 to 10 minutes for medium-rare meat or for 13 to 15 minutes for medium-well meat. Remove the lamb from the pan and let it rest on a cutting board for about 10 minutes before slicing.

11. Slice the lamb into thin pieces for serving. Arrange the slices on each of 4 serving plates and put the root vegetables next to the lamb. Reheat the sauce gently over medium heat. Strain the sauce through a fine-mesh sieve into a gravy boat or serving jug. Pass the sauce on the side.

Basil and Apple–Marinated Organic Chicken

SHERYL: *I'm sure a number of you have seen the many different programs and documentaries depicting the life of commercially raised chickens. It is horrifying to me to think that the inhumane treatment of these animals would ever be a part of our dining experience, and so we make every attempt to eat free-range chicken that is steroid free. Since I started eating free-range, organic chicken, I can't imagine going back to "supermarket birds." And it really matters to me that my two boys will grow up knowing the difference intrinsically, but also that they will not be ingesting the kinds of chemicals that these birds are shot up with to make them grow bigger faster. That is the philosophy I embrace across the board when it comes to meat, in general. Besides, there is far more flavor and far less fat in these than in other chickens.*

Chuck serves this dish with baked polenta, which is warm, firm, and comforting in the winter and mingles deliciously with the chicken juices, the Apple-Fennel Slaw, and the Haricots Verts Salad. A full meal on a plate where every element is meant for the other. Thanks, Chuck, for these amazing flavors and textures. Serves 4

CHICKEN

1½ cups apple juice, preferably organic

2 tablespoons basil pesto, homemade or store-bought

Kosher salt and freshly ground black pepper

4 good-size boneless, skinless chicken breast halves,
    preferably organic and free-range

POLENTA

1½ tablespoons canola oil, preferably expeller-pressed

½ medium yellow onion, diced

1 teaspoon chopped garlic

½ cup white wine

3 cups vegetable stock, homemade or store-bought

1 cup nonfat milk

1½ cups uncooked polenta (preferably not instant)

1 tablespoon extra-virgin olive oil

1 tablespoon chopped flat-leaf parsley

1 tablespoon chopped fresh basil leaves

1 tablespoon chopped fresh oregano

Canola oil, preferably expeller-pressed

CIDER GRAVY

1½ tablespoons canola oil, preferably expeller-pressed

2 tablespoons all-purpose flour

1½ cups organic apple cider

Kosher salt and freshly ground black pepper

TO SERVE

1 recipe Haricots Verts Salad, page 166

1 recipe Apple-Fennel Slaw, page 214

1. To marinate the chicken: In a large zipped plastic bag, combine the apple juice and pesto and season to taste with salt and pepper. Add the chicken breasts and move them around in the bag to coat well with the marinade. Expel the air from the bag and zip it closed. Refrigerate for at least 4 hours and up to 12 hours. Turn the bag every 2 hours or so to ensure the chicken is evenly covered. (Alternatively, marinate the chicken in a shallow, nonreactive dish, turning the chicken several times to ensure it's coated evenly. Keep the dish covered and in the refrigerator.)

2. To make the polenta: Preheat the oven to 350°F. Line a baking sheet with aluminum foil and lightly oil the foil.

3. In a good-size saucepan, heat the oil over medium-high heat and when hot, sauté the onion and garlic for 2 to 3 minutes or until the onion softens. Take care the garlic does not burn. Add the wine, bring to a boil, and cook at the boil for 6 to 8 minutes or until the wine reduces by half.

4. Add the stock and milk and bring to a rapid simmer. Watch carefully so that the liquid does not boil over and adjust the heat up or down to maintain the simmer.

5. With the liquid simmering, slowly add the polenta, whisking as you do. When all is

added, reduce the heat to medium-low and cook, stirring almost constantly, for 10 to 12 minutes or until the polenta is soft and cooked through.

6. Remove polenta from heat and fold in the olive oil, parsley, basil, and oregano.

7. Pour the polenta onto the prepared baking sheet and spread evenly over the pan so that the polenta is about $1/2$-inch thick. Set aside to cool completely.

8. To make the gravy: In a medium-size saucepan, heat the oil on medium heat and when hot, stir the flour into it to make a roux, or paste. Cook the roux for 2 to 3 minutes, stirring occasionally, until the mixture turns a light brown.

9. Whisk the apple cider into the roux to avoid clumping. The gravy should be thick enough to coat the back of a wooden spoon. If the gravy is too thick, whisk in more apple cider. Season with salt and pepper to taste and set aside, covered, to keep warm.

10. To make the chicken: Prepare a gas or charcoal grill so that the heating elements or charcoal are medium-hot. Before you start the fire, rub the grate with a little canola oil to prevent sticking. (Alternatively, heat a grill pan on the stovetop.)

11. Lift the chicken from the marinade and let most of it drip back into the bag or dish. Grill for 10 to 12 minutes, turning at least once, until the chicken breasts are cooked through. Let the chicken breasts rest for a few minutes and then slice each breast into slices, each approximately $1/2$-inch thick.

12. To serve, ladle 2 to 3 tablespoons of gravy on one side of a warm serving plate and top with a spoonful of polenta. Top the polenta with chicken slices. Put some slaw on the plate and a serving of the haricots verts salad next to it.

Miso-Marinated Sea Bass with Orange Ponzu Sauce

CHUCK: *Just a few years ago, sea bass was in danger of extinction, but careful fishing restrictions and responsible husbandry of the supply were so successful, the fish is enthusiastically rebounding. Sheryl and I couldn't be happier, because she now loves eating fish and I love cooking it. The miso marinade for this is incredible and gives the fish a light, refreshing flavor that has folks ooohing and aaahing whenever this is on the menu. I serve this with ponzu sauce made with orange juice rather than the more typical lemon juice, and while you can buy ponzu sauce in Asian markets and on the shelves in the supermarket devoted to Asian ingredients, it's so much better homemade—and very easy.* Serves 4

SEA BASS

½ cup white miso paste

2 tablespoons rice vinegar

Four 6- to 7-ounce center-cut sea bass fillets

ORANGE PONZU SAUCE

1 cup soy sauce

⅔ cup freshly squeezed orange juice

⅓ cup freshly squeezed lime juice

3 tablespoons rice vinegar

2 tablespoons raw or light brown sugar

TO SERVE

1 recipe Cashew Sticky Rice, page 231

1 recipe Spicy Snow Peas, page 223

1. To prepare the sea bass: In a bowl, whisk together the miso paste, ⅓ cup water, and the rice vinegar. Put sea bass in a large zipped bag and pour the marinade over it. Move the fish in the bag to ensure it's well coated. Extract the air from the bag, zip it closed, and refrigerate for at least 3 hours and up to 5 hours. Turn the bag every hour or so to make sure the fish is evenly covered with the

marinade. (Alternatively, marinate the sea bass in a shallow, nonreactive dish, turning the fish several times to ensure it's coated evenly. Keep the dish covered and in the refrigerator.)

2. To make the ponzu sauce: In a medium bowl, whisk together the soy sauce, orange juice, lime juice, vinegar, and sugar, and set aside.

3. Meanwhile, preheat the oven to 425°F. Line a baking sheet with aluminum foil and lightly oil the foil.

4. Lift the sea bass from the marinade and let most of the marinade drip back into the bag or dish. Lay the fish on the baking sheet and roast for 12 to 15 minutes or until the moisture on the inside of the fish starts to bubble to the surface and the bass is cooked through.

5. To serve, put about ³/₄ cup of the rice on each plate and then a serving of the snow peas next to it. Arrange the fish on the plate next to the vegetables and drizzle the ponzu sauce over the fish and around the plate and serve.

White Wine and Herb–Poached Halibut

CHUCK: *Poaching is a delicate cooking technique that yields phenomenal results—and one that is too often overlooked. For the halibut, I pair white wine with aromatic herbs, lemon zest, and garlic for a heady broth that infuses the fish with gentle flavor. Make sure the herbs are fresh and not chopped into small pieces.*

When you poach fish, you can rest easy that it won't ever be dry; plus there's a margin for error with the method that makes it hard to overcook the fish if you are just reasonably diligent. The trickiest part is removing the fillets from the poaching liquid without breaking them—I suggest you use a large slotted spoon or a wide, flexible spatula. I have paired the fish with some nice fall components that are comforting without being the least bit heavy. Serves 4

One 750-ml bottle dry white wine

1 cup vegetable stock or water

8 to 10 whole peppercorns

Grated zest of 1 lemon

3 whole cloves garlic, peeled and lightly smashed with the side of a chef's knife

2 bay leaves

2 teaspoons kosher or sea salt

2 teaspoons honey

¼ cup whole flat-leaf parsley sprigs

¼ cup whole fresh oregano sprigs

¼ cup whole fresh thyme sprigs

4 fillets halibut or any firm white fish, 1 to 1½ inches thick

TO SERVE

1 recipe Carrot-Parsnip Puree, page 215

1 recipe Brussels Sprouts Sauté, page 216

1. In a medium saucepan, bring the wine and stock to a boil over medium-high heat and boil for about 2 minutes. Reduce the heat so that the liquid simmers. Add peppercorns, lemon zest, garlic, bay leaves, salt, and honey and simmer for 5 minutes.

2. Reduce the heat further and simmer very gently so that there are no bubbles and no steam. Add the parsley, oregano, and thyme sprigs, and simmer for 5 minutes longer, adjusting the heat up or down to maintain a very low simmer.

3. Give the poaching liquid a quick stir and slowly lower the fillets, one by one, into the saucepan. Poach for 10 to 12 minutes or until the fish is opaque in the center and flaky.

4. Line a large plate or platter with paper towels. Very carefully and using a slotted spoon or spatula, remove the fillets from the poaching liquid and set them on the paper towels so they can drain.

5. Put a large spoonful of the carrot puree on each of 4 serving plates. Lay a fillet next to the puree, spoon the Brussels sprouts sauté on the other side of the halibut, and serve.

RACHEL'S TIP

Eating fish *together* with garlic (instead of *separately*) is more effective in lowering cholesterol than eating just one or the other.

Mom's Reconstructed Chili

CHUCK: *I learned to make this big-and-bold-tasting chili from my mom, who made it often when we were kids. Both my mom's family and my dad's made this chili, and so it's no surprise that my sister, Jackie, and I follow the tradition now that we are grown. Of course, when we were young, Mom and Dad made it with beef, but because I am a vegetarian and Sheryl likes to eat as healthfully as possible, I switched out the beef and substituted ground soy. Guess what? You can hardly tell the difference. Made with soy, the chili tastes just as robust and intense as beef-based chili.* Serves 6 to 8

1 tablespoon canola oil, preferably expeller-pressed

1 large yellow onion, diced

1 tablespoon chopped garlic

1 pound ground soy burger alternative

2 teaspoons cumin

1½ tablespoons chili powder

½ teaspoon smoked paprika, optional

½ teaspoon dried red chili flakes

One 12-ounce can light beer, at room temperature

1½ tablespoons low-sodium soy sauce

Two 14- to 15-ounce cans chili hot beans with can juices, preferably organic

Two 14- to 15-ounce cans pinto beans, preferably organic, drained

Two 14- to 15-ounce cans fire-roasted diced tomatoes, preferably organic

2 bay leaves

2 teaspoons dried oregano

Kosher salt and freshly ground black pepper

Fat-free saltines or cornbread for serving, optional

Hot pepper sauce, for serving, optional

1. In a large pot, heat the oil over medium heat and when hot, sauté the onion and garlic for 3 to 4 minutes. Add the ground soy and cook for 1 to 2 minutes, stirring with a wooden spoon to break up the soy further and encourage even

cooking. Add the cumin, chili powder, paprika, and chili flakes and continue to cook, stirring, until the spices are slightly toasted and fragrant, 1 to 2 minutes.

2. Using a wooden spoon to prevent sticking, stir in half of the beer and the soy sauce. Add the rest of the beer and stir to mix.

3. Add the chili hot beans, pinto beans, tomatoes, and 1 cup of water and mix well. Add the bay leaves and oregano and stir to mix.

4. Bring the chili to a low boil over medium-high heat and cook for 10 to 15 minutes, stirring every 5 minutes or so until the stew is well blended. Reduce the heat to low and simmer gently until cooked through, 30 to 40 minutes, until the flavors blend. Stir the chili occasionally during cooking. Adjust the heat up or down to maintain a simmer. Serve hot, with crumbled saltines or cornbread, and some extra hot sauce, if desired.

Grilled Tofu "Parmesan" with Homemade Red Wine–Tomato Sauce

CHUCK: *Sheryl may not be a vegetarian, but she appreciates good meatless meals several times a week, so I try to come up with as many vegetarian main courses as I can. I make sure they are as satisfying as any meal where meat or poultry plays the starring role. In this recipe, marinated tofu is the central attraction: big, bold, and proud. There is nothing wimpy or "crunchy granola" about the grilled tofu with the robust tomato sauce. (In fact, the sauce would be great with either chicken or eggplant that you wanted to cook "parmesan.") I especially like to serve this with quinoa or spelt pasta, and maybe some steamed broccoli with a spritz of lemon juice.* Serves 3 to 4

TOFU

3 tablespoons bottled regular or low-fat Italian dressing

2 tablespoons light soy sauce

1 teaspoon dried oregano

1 teaspoon dried basil

1 teaspoon freshly ground black pepper

½ teaspoon kosher salt

1-pound block extra-firm tofu, pressed (see Try Cooking with Tofu on page 18), cut into ½-inch-thick slices

RED WINE–TOMATO SAUCE

1 tablespoon extra-virgin olive oil

1 medium onion, diced

1 tablespoon chopped garlic

One 6-ounce can organic tomato paste

⅔ cup red wine

Two 12-ounce cans crushed organic tomatoes

4 to 5 ripe Roma tomatoes, roughly diced

2 teaspoons dried oregano

2 teaspoons dried basil

2 teaspoons dried thyme

2 bay leaves

1 tablespoon raw or granulated sugar

Kosher salt and freshly ground black pepper

About ½ pound soy mozzarella cheese or dairy mozzarella, cut into ½-inch-thick slices

1. To prepare the tofu: In a mixing bowl, whisk together the Italian dressing, soy sauce, oregano, basil, pepper, and salt. Put the tofu in a shallow glass or ceramic dish or sealable plastic bag and pour the marinade over it. Refrigerate for at least 3 hours and up to 8 hours.

2. To make the sauce: In a medium-size pot, heat the olive oil over medium-high heat and when hot, sauté the onion and garlic until they begin to soften, 2 to 3 minutes. Take care not to burn the garlic. Stir in the tomato paste and cook for 1 to 2 minutes longer.

3. Add the red wine, bring to a boil, and cook for 2 to 3 minutes. Reduce the heat to a simmer and add the crushed tomatoes, Roma tomatoes, oregano, basil, thyme, bay leaves, and sugar. Stir well and season to taste with salt and pepper.

4. Adjust the heat and simmer the sauce until the flavors meld and the sauce thickens slightly, 30 to 40 minutes. Remove the bay leaves and with an immersion blender or handheld electric mixer, blend the sauce until smooth.

5. Serve immediately or refrigerate, covered, for up to 2 weeks.

6. Meanwhile, prepare a gas or charcoal grill so that the heating elements or charcoal are medium-hot. Before you start the fire, rub the grate with a little canola oil to prevent sticking.

7. Using a metal spatula, lift the tofu from the marinade and let any excess liquid drip back into the dish. Grill for 2 to 3 minutes on each side or until lightly charred. (Alternatively, cook the tofu in a nonstick skillet or griddle pan over medium-high heat for 2 to 3 minutes on each side.)

8. Divide the slices of tofu among 3 or 4 serving plates. Top with mozzarella and then ladle about 1/2 cup of the warm sauce over the cheese.

RACHEL'S TIP

Tomatoes are actually more healthful cooked than they are raw. Heat releases lycopene from the tomato's fibers and a touch of olive oil aids its absorption. That makes tomato soups and sauces great (and tasty!) health treats.

Slow-Cooked Salsa Chicken Tacos

CHUCK: *I have made these for Wyatt and a few other kids, who were wild for the tacos. It takes a few hours to cook the chicken so that it's so tender it practically falls apart on its own, but it's so easy—all you need is time. I suggest this for a weekend when you're home, or housebound because of a snowstorm.* Serves 4

CHICKEN

1½ cups chicken stock, preferably organic

One 12-ounce jar mild salsa, preferably organic

2 good-size boneless, skinless chicken breast halves, preferably organic and free-range

TACOS AND TOPPINGS

8 taco shells or soft wheat tortillas, preferably sprouted-grain tortillas

About 2 cups shredded lettuce

About 1 cup diced tomatoes

About 1 cup shredded cheddar or provolone cheese

4 to 6 tablespoons sour cream

1. In a large saucepan, bring the stock and salsa to a simmer over medium heat. Add the chicken and simmer, covered, until the chicken is very tender, about 2 hours.

2. Lift the chicken from the cooking liquid and let it cool for 30 to 40 minutes. Reserve the cooking liquid. When the chicken is cool, shred the meat between your fingers.

3. Transfer the shredded chicken to a bowl and drizzle the reserved cooking liquid over it to keep it moist.

4. Fill the taco shells or tortillas with the chicken and garnish with the toppings of your choice.

> **RACHEL'S TIP**
>
> Sprouted grains are even mightier than standard whole grains. They contain enzymes that make the nutrients easier to digest and absorb. (Plus, they give breads a stylish touch.)

Mostly Vegetarian Lasagna

CHUCK: *I make this lasagna without noodles, so I could be accused of "faking it." But it tastes fantastic, is naturally low in carbohydrates, and all the veggies make it super-healthful. When I serve it, no one complains about the absence of the wide noodles. Wyatt gobbles it up, so I guess that makes it kid friendly!* Serves 6 to 8

3 to 4 zucchini, thinly sliced lengthwise

2 teaspoons canola oil, preferably expeller-pressed

Salt

1 tablespoon olive oil

1 pound ground organic turkey Italian sausage (I use Jennie-O
   or Applegate Farms brands)

½ cup diced onion

1 teaspoon chopped garlic

1½ cups diced yellow summer squash

1½ cups diced portobello mushrooms

1 teaspoon dried basil

1 teaspoon dried oregano

6 cups Red Wine–Tomato Sauce (page 206) or jarred tomato sauce

4 cups low-fat ricotta cheese

½ cup grated parmesan cheese

2 cups shredded mozzarella cheese

1. Preheat the oven to 350°F.
2. In a large bowl, toss the sliced zucchini with the canola oil. Spread the zucchini on 2 baking sheets and bake to dry out slightly, 4 to 5 minutes. Transfer the zucchini to paper towels and sprinkle slightly with salt. (The zucchini will replace the more traditional noodles, and this keeps the lasagna pleasingly dry, not watery, when it's assembled.)
3. Raise the oven temperature to 375°F. Grease a 13 x 9-inch baking pan.
4. In a medium-size pot, heat the olive oil over medium heat. When hot, cook the turkey sausage until lightly browned, stirring and breaking it up with a wooden spoon. Add the onion and garlic and cook for 1 to 2 minutes, stirring.

Add the squash, mushrooms, basil, and oregano. Cook, stirring, until the vegetables soften, 4 to 5 minutes longer. Remove the pan from the heat and set aside to cool.

5. Ladle about 1½ cups of tomato sauce into the pan and spread it evenly. Layer a third of the zucchini over the sauce in an even layer and top with half of the sausage mixture. Ladle another 1½ cups of sauce over the turkey in an even layer.

6. Spoon the ricotta into a pastry bag or a plastic bag with a corner snipped off. Pipe the cheese evenly over the sauce. Top with another third of the zucchini slices. Repeat layering with sauce, turkey mixture, more sauce, and ricotta.

7. Layer the remaining zucchini slices over the ricotta. Sprinkle with the parmesan cheese and then with the shredded mozzarella.

8. Bake for 40 to 45 minutes or until the lasagna is bubbling hot. Let the casserole cool slightly and then serve.

Side Dishes

Apple-Fennel Slaw

CHUCK: *There is something about fennel, which is at its best in the fall and winter, that makes it a natural with sweet, tart apples. This is one of my favorite combinations, which tastes terrific with just about anything grilled or pan-seared. I serve it with the chicken on page 195.* Serves 4

1 large bulb of fennel, trimmed of feathery fronds
1 cup organic apple juice
1 large red apple
1 tablespoon chopped flat-leaf parsley
2 teaspoons olive oil
Kosher salt and freshly ground black pepper

1. Cut about $\frac{1}{2}$ inch from the bottom of the trimmed fennel bulb. Cut the bulb in half and then into very thin slices.
2. Transfer the slices to a glass or other nonreactive container. Add the apple juice, cover, and refrigerate to allow the fennel to soak for at least 1 hour and up to 2 hours.
3. Just before serving, peel and core the apple. Cut it in half and then into thin slices, about the size of the fennel slices.
4. Drain the apple juice from the fennel. Add the apple slices and parsley to the fennel and dress with the olive oil. Toss gently, season to taste with salt and pepper, and serve. (Be sure to serve this no more than 1 hour after tossing, or the apples will begin to turn brown.)

RACHEL'S TIP

Fennel is one multi-talented vegetable. Not only is it rich in fiber, vitamin C, folate, and potassium, it's also a superstar stomach calmer and de-bloater.

Carrot-Parsnip Puree

CHUCK: *Both carrots and parsnips are sweet root vegetables that somehow complement each other more than other combinations—plus their natural colors mimic those of the woods in the fall, which makes them perfect for the changing season. Purees are soothing and elegant, and so I tend to make them in the dark, cold months.* Serves 4

3 cups low-fat milk or soy milk

3 medium-to-large parsnips, peeled and cut into even pieces (about 1½ cups)

2 medium-to-large carrots, peeled and cut into even pieces (about 1 cup)

2 tablespoons unsalted butter or soy butter

Kosher salt and freshly ground black pepper

1. In a medium-size saucepan, bring the milk, parsnips, and carrots to a boil, reduce to a simmer, and cook for 20 to 25 minutes or until very tender but not quite mushy. The vegetables should be fully submerged. If there is not enough liquid to cover them, add more milk. Also watch that the liquid does not boil over. Adjust the heat up or down to maintain a simmer.

2. With a slotted spoon, transfer the parsnips and carrots into a blender. Add ½ cup of the milk broth to the blender and puree on medium-low speed. Without pushing the vegetables all the way into the blender, so that they hit the blades at the bottom of the blender, slowly press on the vegetables until they begin to puree. If the puree is too thick, add more milk, ¼ cup at a time, until you achieve the consistency of baby food.

3. Add the butter and season to taste with salt and pepper. Serve warm or reheat in the microwave if necessary for 30 to 45 seconds.

Brussels Sprouts Sauté

SHERYL: *Believe it or not, I have come to love Brussels sprouts, especially when they are fresh from the farmers' market. This is one of those foods that my nutritionist, Rachel, would always tout as being high in antioxidant properties— boosted here with the addition of the cauliflower, it's definitely a "feel good" dish!*
Serves 4

Note: To toast the pine nuts, spread them in a small, dry skillet or sauté pan and heat them over medium heat, shaking the pan until the seeds are fragrant and darken a shade, 2 or 3 minutes. Transfer the seeds to a separate dish to cool.

1½ cups cauliflower florets

4 teaspoons canola oil, preferably expeller-pressed

Kosher salt and freshly ground black pepper

1 pint Brussels sprouts

⅓ cup currants or raisins

¼ cup toasted pine nuts, see Note

¼ cup white wine

1 tablespoon unsalted butter

1 tablespoon chopped flat-leaf parsley

1. Preheat the oven to 400°F.
2. In a large bowl, toss the cauliflower with 1 teaspoon of the oil and salt and pepper to taste. Spread the cauliflower on a lightly greased baking sheet and roast for 10 to 12 minutes or until lightly browned and softened. Set aside.
3. Rinse and then trim the Brussels sprouts. Separate the leaves from the heads and transfer them to a cup measure. You will have about 2 cups of leaves.
4. In a large sauté pan, heat the remaining 3 teaspoons of the oil over medium-high heat and when hot and shimmering, add the Brussels sprout leaves, cauliflower, currants, and pine nuts and cook, stirring, for 1 to 2 minutes.
5. Add the wine and cook for 1 more minute. Remove from the heat and stir in the butter and parsley until the butter melts. Season to taste with salt and pepper.

Red Wine–Braised Cabbage with Caraway Seeds

SHERYL: *My mom used to make slaw with purple cabbage, but not until I began working with Chuck and Rachel on incorporating immune-boosting foods into my diet did I realize the benefits of eating the purple cabbage over the more commonly used white cabbage. It is super-healthful and yummy, and I have made it a part of my normal diet.* Serves 6 to 8

> 1 medium head purple cabbage
> 1 tablespoon canola oil, preferably expeller-pressed
> 1 medium yellow onion, thinly sliced (about 1½ cups)
> 1 tablespoon chopped garlic
> 1⅓ tablespoons caraway seeds
> One 750-ml bottle red wine (something that you would drink)
> Kosher salt and freshly ground black pepper
> 3 tablespoons unsalted butter

1. Remove the tough outer leaves from the head of cabbage. Cut the head in half and remove the core. With a large knife, slice the cabbage into thin strips or shreds. You will have 6 or 7 cups of cabbage.

2. In a large saucepan, heat the oil over medium-high heat and when hot sauté the onion for about 1 minute. Add the garlic and continue to cook for 1 to 2 minutes, taking care the garlic does not burn. Add the caraway seeds and stir them in the pan for 30 to 40 seconds to allow them to toast a little.

3. Add the red wine, bring to a boil, and cook for 2 to 3 minutes. Add the cabbage to the pan and gently fold it into the liquid. Salt the cabbage with a good-size pinch of salt to draw moisture out of the cabbage. Season lightly with pepper. Cook for 20 to 25 minutes, stirring every 5 minutes or so, or until the cabbage wilts. Reduce the heat and simmer gently for 20 to 25 minutes longer, stirring once or twice. Taste and add more salt and pepper if needed.

4. Just before serving, stir in the butter and when melted and well incorporated, serve the cabbage.

Cauliflower "Mashed Potatoes" with Caramelized Onions

SHERYL: *If you like mashed potatoes, try this—it's just as tasty . . . and it's so much better for you than the spuds. Cauliflower, a close cousin of broccoli, is crammed with vitamins C and K, folate, potassium, and phytochemicals that may reduce the risk of some cancers. If you are like me, you'd be happy to eat mashed potatoes with every meal. This is a great substitute!* Serves 4 to 6

1 tablespoon canola oil, preferably expeller-pressed

2 yellow onions, halved and sliced thinly

½ cup low-fat milk or unsweetened plain soy milk

2 heads cauliflower, cut into florets with tender portions of stem attached

3 tablespoons unsalted butter or soy butter

2 teaspoons garlic powder

1 teaspoon freshly squeezed lemon juice

Kosher salt and freshly ground black pepper

1. In a deep, medium-size pot, heat the oil over medium-low heat and when hot, cook the onions very slowly until caramelized, 15 to 20 minutes.
2. Add the milk and bring to a boil over medium-high heat. When boiling, add the cauliflower, stir to mix, cover, and cook for 2 to 3 minutes. Remove the lid and continue to cook for 2 to 3 minutes longer or until most of the liquid has evaporated.
3. Remove the pot from the heat and add the butter, garlic powder, and lemon juice. Season to taste with salt and pepper.
4. Using a potato masher or heavy fork, mash the cauliflower thoroughly. (For a smoother consistency, puree the mixture in the bowl of a food processor fitted with the metal blade.)
5. Reheat the mashed cauliflower gently over medium-low heat before serving.

Roasted Root Vegetables

SHERYL: *Nothing makes a house smell more like a home than the smell of home cooking. I smell roasting root veggies long before I see them. The aroma wafts from the kitchen down to my studio, making us smile in anticipation of Chuck's meal to come. All these vegetables are easy to get in the cold months; roasting them, Chuck tells me, brings out their natural sweetness and gorgeous flavors.* Serves 4 to 5

2 medium-size red potatoes, not peeled (about ½ pound)

1 large carrot, peeled

1 large parsnip, peeled

1 medium-size turnip, peeled

⅓ cup diced fennel

¼ cup diced red onion

1½ tablespoons canola oil, preferably expeller-pressed

2 teaspoons garlic powder

Kosher salt and freshly ground black pepper

2 tablespoons chopped flat-leaf parsley

1. Preheat the oven to 425°F. Line a baking sheet with aluminum foil and lightly oil the foil.
2. Cut the potatoes, carrot, parsnip, and turnip into even-size dice, about ¼ inch across. Transfer the vegetables to a large mixing bowl and add the fennel and onion. Toss with the oil and garlic powder and season to taste with salt and pepper. Toss well.
3. Spread the vegetables in a relatively even layer on the baking sheet and roast until the vegetables are tender and crispy, 23 to 25 minutes. Stir them about halfway through roasting to ensure even cooking. Serve the vegetables garnished with the parsley.

Pickled Red Onions

CHUCK: *Red onions are naturally sweet, but when they're raw, they can taste sharp. To counteract this, I brine them with a simple mixture of vinegar and sugar for an easy sweet-and-sour relish—great on sandwiches, with salads, or to accompany cold meats and cheese, and such a cool color, too. In this book, I serve them with the Mixed Lettuces with Anjou Pears, Toasted Walnuts, Blue Cheese, and Pickled Red Onions (page 165) and with the Bruschetta with Tofu Spread and Summer Vegetables (page 17).* Makes about 1 cup

> 1 medium red onion, peeled, halved, and julienned or thinly sliced
>
> 1 cup water
>
> 1½ cups red wine vinegar
>
> 1 tablespoon kosher salt
>
> 1½ tablespoons sugar

1. Put the sliced onion in a glass, ceramic, or other nonreactive bowl large enough to hold it without crowding, but not so big it is lost in the bowl.

2. In a small saucepan, combine 1 cup of water with the vinegar, salt, and sugar. Bring to a boil over medium-high heat. When the pickling liquid comes to a boil, pour it over the onions, making sure to cover them completely. If not, transfer the onions and liquid to a smaller bowl. Give the onions a stir and set aside at room temperature for 4 hours.

3. Cover and refrigerate until ready to serve. The pickles will keep for up to 2 weeks.

Spicy Snow Peas

CHUCK: *Because I can find snow peas at the market all year long, I often make them in the wintertime when a fresh vegetable goes a long way. If you can't find them fresh, buy them frozen. Today's quick-frozen vegetables are nearly as healthful as fresh, and some might argue they are more beneficial, as they retain more of their naturally occurring vitamins. The red chili flakes, garlic, and ginger give these an Asian flair and welcome zing.* Serves 4

> 2 teaspoons soy butter or unsalted butter
>
> 1 teaspoon chopped garlic
>
> 1 teaspoon chopped fresh ginger
>
> ¼ teaspoon dried red chili flakes
>
> 1½ cups trimmed snow peas
>
> Kosher salt and freshly ground black pepper

1. Heat a large sauté pan over heat and melt the butter. When it's hot and melted, add the garlic, ginger, and chili flakes and sauté for 30 to 45 seconds or just until fragrant.
2. Add the snow peas and continue to sauté for 2 to 3 minutes longer or until the peas soften slightly. Season the peas with salt and pepper to taste, remove from the heat, and serve immediately or cover to keep warm.

Lentils with Sage, Roasted Garlic, and Parsnips

CHUCK: *I love to cook lentils for any number of reasons, not the least being that they cook quickly and don't require soaking first, as do other dried legumes. For this dish, you can use just about any kind of lentil you want—green, brown, or red. As tasty as the lentils are, the secret ingredient in this dish is the parsnips. These close cousins to the carrot are a little sweet with a pleasingly starchy consistency and so add flavor and texture that may be a little hard to place for a lot of people, but will make everyone happy.* Serves 4 to 6

  1 tablespoon canola oil, preferably expeller-pressed

  1 medium yellow onion, diced

  ½ pound fresh parsnips, peeled and grated (about 1 cup)

  ¾ cup chopped cooked bacon or chopped cooked Smart Bacon (about 3 slices)

  1½ cups vegetable stock, preferably organic

  2 tablespoons chopped roasted garlic, see How to Roast Garlic, opposite

  1 bay leaf

  1 cup dried green, brown, or red lentils

  1½ tablespoons unsalted butter

  1 tablespoon fresh chopped sage leaves

  Kosher salt and freshly ground black pepper

1. In a medium-size pot, heat the canola oil over medium heat and when hot, sauté the onion until it begins to soften, 2 to 3 minutes. Add the grated parsnip and chopped bacon and sauté until well incorporated, 1 to 2 minutes.

2. Add the vegetable stock, roasted garlic, and bay leaf and bring to a boil over medium-high heat. Add the lentils, bring the liquid back to a boil, and cook for 4 to 5 minutes. Reduce the heat so that the liquid simmers and cook until the lentils are soft but not mushy, 15 to 20 minutes.

3. Drain any excess liquid. Add the butter and sage, stir well, and season to taste with salt and pepper.

HOW TO ROAST GARLIC

There are several different ways to roast garlic and the end result is always the same: mild, soft, and full flavored—very unlike raw garlic. Once you try it, you'll be convinced the little bit of effort offers great rewards. The rich flavor complements so many dishes and the mildness makes it far easier to eat healthful amounts of the pungent bulb.

Here is one of the easiest methods for roasting garlic:

Start with a full head (or more) and peel off the outer papery layers of skin. Leave the cloves intact as you do this. With a large, sharp knife, cut about ¼ to ½ inch off the top of the head to expose the top of the garlic cloves. Put the head (or heads), with the exposed top facing up, in a small baking pan or dish and drizzle a few teaspoons of olive oil over the head. Rub the oil over the garlic so that the head is well covered.

Cover the dish with aluminum foil and then bake in a pre-heated 400°F oven for 30 to 35 minutes or until the cloves feel soft when pressed. Let the garlic head (or heads) cool and then squeeze the roasted pulp from the individual cloves and discard the skin. You can now use the garlic as you need it: mashed, diced, or spread over a slice of warm French bread.

Braised Winter Greens with Fried Pumpkin and Feta

CHUCK: *Greens such as chard, kale, and collards grow in happy abundance and are easy to find in supermarkets and at farmers' markets and greengrocers all across the country. Back in the day, these winter greens were sometimes called "cooking greens"; they are not especially digestible or appetizing unless they are cooked until wilted. And don't worry if the tumble of leaves in the pan looks enormous: They wilt down very handily. When they're cooked, these greens are outstanding—full of flavor and even fuller of nutrients.*

This is a dish you would only make in the late fall or winter—think Thanksgiving. Greens and fried pumpkin: What a terrific duo. A word of warning: Use small, fleshy pumpkins for cooking, such as Sugar Pie and Baby Bear. Large field pumpkins are best left for Halloween jack-o'-lanterns. Serves 4 to 6

WINTER GREENS

1½ tablespoons canola oil, preferably expeller-pressed

1 large yellow onion, thinly sliced

1½ tablespoons chopped garlic

1 teaspoon dried red chili flakes

1½ cups vegetable broth, preferably organic

3 pounds assorted winter greens, such as Swiss chard, kale, turnip greens, mustard greens, or collards, leaves torn from stems and stems sliced thinly

2 tablespoons apple cider vinegar

Kosher salt

FRIED PUMPKIN

1 cup canola oil, preferably expeller-pressed

1½ cup diced, peeled pumpkin

Kosher salt and freshly ground black pepper

TO SERVE

¼ cup feta cheese

1. To cook the greens: In a large pot, heat the canola oil over medium-high heat and when hot, sauté the onion and garlic until softened, 2 to 3 minutes. Add the chili flakes and continue to cook for about 1 minute.

2. Add the broth and bring to a boil. Reduce the heat so that the broth simmers. Put half of the greens in the pot, mixing them with long tongs. When the first half of the greens wilts, add the rest. When these wilt, simmer for about 30 minutes, stirring occasionally, until tender. Adjust the heat to maintain a slow simmer.

3. Drain the greens and return them to the pot. Add the vinegar and salt, stir well, and cover to keep warm.

4. To fry the pumpkin: In a large frying pan, heat the oil over medium-high heat. The oil should be $1/2$ inch deep. To test if the oil is hot enough for frying, sprinkle the oil with water and if it sizzles, the oil is hot. The air above the oil will shimmer.

5. Working in 2 batches, fry half of the diced pumpkin, making sure to turn it in the oil with a long-handled spoon or tongs so that it is crispy on all sides. Fry the pumpkin for 3 to 4 minutes or until tender. Lift the pumpkin from the oil with a slotted spoon and drain on a plate lined with paper towels. Season lightly with salt and pepper. Repeat with the rest of the pumpkin,

6. Put the greens in a serving bowl and top with the fried pumpkin. Sprinkle with the feta cheese and serve.

Quick Red Cabbage Sauerkraut

CHUCK: *You may never have thought of making your own sauerkraut, but why not? This is great on sandwiches and alongside cooked sausages and tangy cheeses. I especially like it with the Vegan Reuben (page 141). It's a quick version of the "real thing" and I intentionally made it with red, or purple, cabbage because it is a good source of antioxidants.* Serves 6 to 8; makes 2½ to 3 cups

1 medium head red or purple cabbage, cored and shredded (7 to 8 cups)

1 tablespoon canola oil, preferably expeller-pressed

1 medium onion, thinly sliced

1¼ cups rice wine vinegar

½ cup apple cider

1 tablespoon kosher salt

2 teaspoons caraway seeds

1 teaspoon garlic powder

1 teaspoon freshly ground black pepper

1. Put the shredded cabbage in a large colander and rinse well. Let it drain.

1. In a large saucepan, heat the oil over medium heat and when hot, sauté the onion for 3 to 4 minutes. Add the cabbage, vinegar, cider, salt, caraway seeds, garlic powder, and pepper and stir well. Reduce the heat to medium-low and let the sauerkraut cook for about 40 minutes, stirring every 7 to 8 minutes.

1. Remove from the heat and transfer the sauerkraut to a shallow pan. Spread the cabbage out into as thin a layer as possible and let it cool a little. Cover and refrigerate for at least 2 hours.

1. Serve the sauerkraut or refrigerate it for storage in a lidded container or well-sealed plastic bag. It will keep for up to 2 weeks.

> **RACHEL'S TIP**
>
> Sauerkraut is loaded with stomach-friendly, immunity-boosting probiotics. Bonus: not only is all cabbage cancer fighting, but when it comes to antioxidant content, RED is the best!

Curried Couscous

CHUCK: *Although some people think it's a grain, couscous is a pasta and cooks very quickly, which makes it a favorite with home cooks in a hurry. It's eaten throughout northern Africa and countries surrounding the Mediterranean; this recipe showcases its versatility, since in the regions of its origin, couscous is traditionally served with lamb or chicken and almost always as a stew. I mix it with nuts and chickpeas for a curried side dish that could also serve as a meatless main course.* Serves 6 to 8

2 cups whole-wheat couscous

½ teaspoon salt

1½ cups julienned fresh spinach leaves

1½ cups julienned red cabbage (about ¼ of a small head)

1 cup canned chickpeas, preferably organic, drained and rinsed

½ cup dried cranberries

⅓ cup sliced, toasted almonds, see Note on page 166

2 tablespoons chopped cilantro

3 tablespoons extra-virgin olive oil

Juice of 2 lemons (about 2 tablespoons)

Kosher salt and freshly ground black pepper

About 1 tablespoon yellow curry powder

1. Put the couscous in a large glass or ceramic bowl and pour 3 cups of boiling water over it. Add the salt and stir to mix. Cover and let the couscous soak for at least 15 minutes and no longer than 20 minutes. Fluff the couscous with a fork.
2. Add the spinach, cabbage, chickpeas, cranberries, almonds, and cilantro and toss thoroughly. Dress with the olive oil and lemon juice and season to taste with salt and pepper. Toss again thoroughly.
3. Add 1 tablespoon of the curry powder and toss again. Taste and add more curry if needed. Serve warm or at room temperature.

Cashew Sticky Rice

CHUCK: *For the best success with this dish, be sure to buy medium-grain rice. Long-grain rice, which is the most common kind in U.S. markets, cooks into the light, fluffy rice we all know and love. The shorter-grained rices are starchier and stickier when cooked. Rices labeled as paella rice or risotto rice are good bets for this.* Serves 4

1 ⅓ cups medium-grain brown rice
2 tablespoons rice vinegar
1 tablespoon soy sauce
2 tablespoons sugar
1 tablespoon salt
1 cup toasted, chopped cashews, see Note
1 bunch scallions, sliced, white and green parts

1. Line a baking sheet with aluminum foil and lightly oil the foil.
2. Wash the rice 2 to 3 times under cold running water to remove excess starch. Drain the rice and then transfer it to a medium-size saucepan and add 2 cups water. Bring to a boil over medium-high heat, and reduce the heat to low so that the rice simmers very slowly. Cover the pan and cook for about 40 minutes or until all the water is absorbed. Do not rush the cooking and adjust the heat up or down to maintain a very low simmer. Remove the pan from the heat and let it stand, covered, for 10 minutes.
3. Pour the rice onto the prepared baking sheet and spread evenly over the pan so that the rice is about ½ inch thick.
4. In a glass measuring cup or similar container, whisk together the vinegar, soy sauce, sugar, and salt. Sprinkle this over the rice and mix the rice gently with a wooden spoon or a sushi paddle to ensure even distribution. Add the cashews and scallions and gently incorporate them into the rice, taking care not to break any grains of rice, if possible. Set aside to cool completely.

Note: To toast the cashews, spread them in a dry skillet and heat them over medium heat, or roast in a 400°F oven, spread on a baking sheet for 6 to 8 minutes or until the cashews darken a few shades.

Barley and Vegetable Risotto

CHUCK: *There is no way around it: Making risotto takes time and attention. But when you have the time, you will be rewarded with an especially creamy, tender dish that will make the rest of the meal a little less important. I make this when the weather outside keeps me in the kitchen and everyone is hungry and eager for a rich, satisfying side dish that pairs nicely with main courses such as roasted chicken or quick, pan-fried fish. I make the risotto with barley rather than rice; like all whole grains, barley is a great source of vitamins, minerals, and amino acids, as well as protein. Plus, barley is an incredible source of both soluble and insoluble fiber. The pan you use to make the risotto should be roomy and heavy so that you have ample room to stir the grains as the liquid is absorbed, and so that they won't scorch from the heat.* Serves 6 to 8

> 2 to 3 asparagus spears, tough stem ends removed or discarded
>
> 3½ cups vegetable stock, preferably organic
>
> 2 tablespoons canola oil, preferably expeller-pressed
>
> 1 medium onion, finely diced
>
> 1 cup pearl barley
>
> 1 tablespoon chopped garlic
>
> 1 cup white wine
>
> ½ cup diced roasted red peppers, preferably organic
>
> 2 tightly packed cups baby spinach
>
> ¼ cup toasted pine nuts, see Note on page 216
>
> ¼ cup grated Parmesan cheese
>
> 2 tablespoons olive oil
>
> 2 teaspoons freshly squeezed lemon juice
>
> 2 teaspoons chopped fresh thyme leaves
>
> Kosher salt and freshly ground black pepper

1. Cut the asparagus into 1-inch-long pieces, including the tips. You should have about ¾ cup of asparagus. Fill a bowl with ice and water and set near the stove.
2. In a large saucepan filled with boiling, salted water, blanch the asparagus for 2 to 3 minutes or until the asparagus turns bright green and begins to soften.

Drain well and submerge the asparagus in the ice water to stop the cooking. Drain again.

3. In a medium-size saucepan, bring the vegetable stock to a simmer over medium-high heat. Reduce the heat to medium-low and hold at a very gentle simmer. Adjust the heat to maintain the simmer.

4. Meanwhile, in a large, heavy saucepan, heat the canola oil over medium-high heat and when hot, sauté the onion until it begins to soften, 2 to 3 minutes. Add the barley and garlic and stir well to make sure they are well coated with oil and the barley toasts slightly. Cook for 2 to 3 minutes. Add the white wine and cook until all liquid is absorbed by the barley.

5. Add the simmering vegetable stock, $^1/_2$ cup at a time, and stir slowly. Do not add the next ladleful of stock until the first is completely absorbed by the barley. This will take about 50 minutes. Once the vegetable stock has been absorbed, check to make sure the barley is tender. If not, add water, $^1/_4$ cup at a time, until tender.

6. Remove the risotto from the heat and fold in the asparagus, roasted red peppers, spinach, pine nuts, Parmesan cheese, olive oil, lemon juice, and thyme. Season well with salt and pepper and serve immediately.

Brown Basmati Rice with Soy-Sage Sausage and Roasted Mushrooms

CHUCK: *These roasted mushrooms are very easy to cook and taste so good, you might find yourself roasting them to add to other dishes, too. The oven-roasting method works with just about any kind of mushroom that looks appealing and plump in the market—and I suggest you buy smooth-looking 'shrooms, regardless of the kind. Sheryl and I like this with soy-sage sausage, but if you prefer pork or beef sausage, go for it. Any kind of sausage adds good flavor to the rice and mushrooms. A quick word of warning: Don't salt the mushrooms before you roast them, as the salt will draw needed moisture from them.* Serves 6 to 8

ROASTED MUSHROOMS

3 cups sliced assorted fresh mushrooms, such as crimini, button, shiitake, and oyster

2½ tablespoons canola oil, preferably expeller-pressed

1½ tablespoons soy sauce

2 teaspoons dried thyme

Freshly ground black pepper

Kosher salt

RICE

1½ tablespoons canola oil, preferably expeller-pressed

¾ cup finely diced carrots

½ cup finely diced celery

½ cup finely diced fennel

8 ounces soy-sage sausage meat or cooked organic pork or beef sausage meat

1 tablespoon chopped garlic

2¼ cups vegetable broth, preferably organic

1 bay leaf

1 cup brown basmati rice

1 tablespoon olive oil

1 tablespoon chopped flat-leaf parsley

Kosher salt and freshly ground black pepper

1. Preheat the oven to 425°F. Line a baking sheet with aluminum foil and lightly oil the foil.

2. In a large mixing bowl, toss the mushrooms with the oil, soy sauce, and thyme. Season to taste with pepper and toss gently.

3. Spread the mushrooms on the foil-lined baking sheet and roast for 10 to 12 minutes. Let the mushrooms cool to room temperature and when cool, season to taste with salt. Set aside at room temperature.

4. In a medium-size pot with a tight-fitting lid, heat the canola oil over medium-high heat and when hot, sauté the carrots, celery, and fennel until they begin to soften, 4 to 5 minutes.

5. Add the sausage meat and garlic and cook, stirring, for 2 to 3 minutes longer. Add the broth and bay leaf and bring to a boil.

6. Add the rice to the boiling liquid, stir, and boil for 1 to 2 minutes. Reduce the heat to low, stir again, cover the pot, and simmer the rice for 45 to 50 minutes or until tender and the liquid is absorbed. Remove the pot from the heat and let it sit, still covered, for about 10 minutes. Drain off any excess liquid.

7. To finish, stir in the mushrooms, olive oil, and parsley. Season to taste with salt and pepper and serve at once.

Desserts

Chocolate-Avocado Mousse Martinis with Fresh Raspberries

SHERYL: *I love it when this is on the menu because it appeases any craving I might have for chocolate. And you would never have guessed that Chuck used avocado to thicken the mousse and that it would make it so delicious. Avocados are mild and sweet enough to blend seamlessly with the chocolate. This is super-healthful: no eggs, no cream, no white sugar in this mousse, and yet it's absolutely glorious.* Serves 3 to 4

2 large ripe avocados
½ cup organic unsweetened cocoa powder (I like Green & Black's organic
    fair trade cocoa powder)
½ cup agave nectar, plus more to taste
1½ teaspoons pure vanilla extract
1½ teaspoons almond extract
½ pint fresh raspberries, for garnish

1. Halve and pit the avocados and scoop out the flesh. Transfer the avocado flesh to the bowl of a food processor fitted with the metal blade. Using a spoon, break up the avocado a little in the food processor.
2. Add the cocoa powder, agave nectar, vanilla extract, and almond extract to the processor and process for 1 to 2 minutes. Scrape down the sides of the bowl and then process again until the mousse is very smooth, 1 to 2 minutes longer.
3. Taste the mousse and if not sweet enough, add more nectar, 1 teaspoon at a time. Pulse to mix.
4. Spoon the mousse into martini glasses or similar serving vessels. Cover the glasses with plastic wrap and refrigerate for at least 1 hour and up to 8 hours.
5. Serve the mousse chilled and garnished with raspberries.

> **RACHEL'S TIP**
>
> Just one ounce of dark chocolate packs as many antioxidants as a glass of red wine. Buy natural cocoa powder with a minimum 70 percent cocoa, and to keep the good stuff (flavonoids), avoiding anything that says "Dutch processed" or "processed with alkali."

Banana Bread Pudding

SHERYL: *I am not that big of a sweet eater: I generally gravitate to salt. But this dessert is one I cannot pass up. I love it because it has all the flavors I adore, particularly banana. There are just some days when we need bread pudding for comfort and soothing. This is one of the best I have ever put in my mouth. Chuck comes through again!* Serves 10 to 12

> 3 cups heavy cream or 2 cups low-fat milk
>
> 1 cup packed light brown sugar
>
> 3 large eggs, preferably omega-3 eggs, lightly beaten
>
> 2 large egg yolks, lightly beaten
>
> 1 tablespoon vanilla extract
>
> 1 teaspoon ground cinnamon
>
> ½ teaspoon salt
>
> 1 large sweet Italian baguette or plain Italian baguette, cut
>   into ½-inch cubes (6 to 7 cups)
>
> 5 to 6 ripe bananas, cut into half-moon slices (about 3 cups)
>
> 1 cup semisweet, milk, or white chocolate chips
>
> ¾ cup toffee chips

1. Preheat the oven to 350°F and grease a 13 x 9-inch glass baking dish.
2. In a large mixing bowl, whisk together the cream, brown sugar, eggs, egg yolks, vanilla, cinnamon, and salt.
3. Add the bread cubes, bananas, chocolate chips, and toffee chips and toss gently. Let the mixture sit for about 5 minutes to give the bread time to absorb the cream and eggs. Toss again until the mixture is completely soggy.
4. Spread the bread pudding in the baking dish, cover with aluminum foil, and bake for 35 to 40 minutes. Remove the foil and bake for another 20 minutes or until the pudding is set but still soft.
5. Serve the pudding cut into squares or rectangles while it is still warm.

Port Wine–Poached Pear with Brandy, Mascarpone, and Walnuts

CHUCK: *When you are lucky enough to come across really good pears—and sadly it's becoming an increasingly rare occurrence these days—eat a few and then poach the rest. This is truly one of the most elegant and yet easiest desserts around, and so good in the wintertime. I team these with a rich creamy filling and some toasted walnuts.* Serves 4

PEARS

One 750-ml bottle port wine

1 cup sugar

5 whole cloves

1 cinnamon stick

4 Anjou or Bosc pears, peeled, cored, and bottoms trimmed

BRANDY MASCARPONE FILLING

One 4-ounce package mascarpone, softened at room temperature
   for at least 2 hours

1½ tablespoons honey

1½ tablespoons brandy

¼ cup chopped toasted walnuts, see Note on page 165

Milk, for thinning the filling, optional

Mint leaves, for garnish, optional

1. To poach the pears: In a medium saucepan, combine the port, 1½ cups water, sugar, cloves, and cinnamon stick and bring to a boil over medium-high heat. Cook for 3 to 4 minutes, and then reduce the heat to medium-low so that the poaching liquid simmers. Submerge the pears in the liquid and weight them with a small pan lid to keep them from bobbing to the surface. The liquid should cover them completely—if not, add a little more water until it does.

2. Poach the pears at a low, gentle simmer until fork tender, about 5 minutes. Remove the pan from the heat and let the pears, still submerged and weighted with the pan lid, cool slightly.

3. Cover the pan and (with the smaller lid still weighting the pears) refrigerate for at least 8 hours and up to 12 hours, or overnight.

4. When the pears have chilled, lift them from the poaching liquid and transfer them to a plate or dish large enough to hold them upright. Cover with plastic wrap and return to the refrigerator.

5. Bring the poaching liquid back to a boil over high heat and boil for 7 to 8 minutes or until reduced by half. Strain through a fine-mesh sieve into a glass container, cover, and refrigerate with the pears for at least 2 hours.

6. To make the filling: In a mixing bowl, vigorously whisk together the cheese, honey, brandy, and walnuts. If the cheese is too thick, add milk or water to it, 1 teaspoon at a time. The filling should not be so thin that it slides off the pears.

7. Spoon the cheese into a pastry bag fitted with a plain tip, or put it in a sturdy plastic bag and refrigerate for least 2 hours and up to 4 hours.

8. To serve, remove the pears from the liquid and set them on a work surface. Pipe the cheese filling into the core of each pear. If you are using a plastic bag, snip away one of the bottom corners of the bag and push on the bag to insert the filling into the pears. (Alternately, thin the mascarpone filling with a little milk and spoon a little on each plate. With the back of the spoon, flatten and spread it out. Set a pear on top.)

9. Spoon 1 tablespoon of the reduced poaching liquid, circling the mascarpone filling. Garnish with a mint leaf, if using, and serve.

Apple-Cranberry Crisp with Vanilla-Almond Granola

CHUCK: *This quick and simple dessert can be turned into a vegan dessert if you serve it with Soy Delicious ice cream or vanilla Rice Dream frozen dessert. If you have apples in the house, you can make this just about at the last minute.* Serves 6 to 8

4 to 5 medium apples, peeled, cored, and sliced thinly (about 4 cups)

⅓ cup dried cranberries

⅓ cup soy butter, softened, or unsalted butter, softened

½ cup packed light brown sugar

½ cup unbleached all-purpose flour

½ cup plain granola

¼ cup roasted almonds, see Note on page 166

2 teaspoons pure vanilla extract

¾ teaspoon ground cinnamon

½ teaspoon salt

Vanilla ice cream, optional

1. Preheat the oven to 375°F. Grease an 8 x 8-inch baking pan.
2. Spread the apple slices and cranberries in the pan in an even layer.
3. In a separate bowl, using your fingers and a fork or wooden spoon, mix together the butter, sugar, flour, granola, almonds, vanilla, cinnamon, and salt. The mixture will be crumbly, not smooth. Spoon the mixture over the fruit, spreading it so that it covers the fruit evenly.
4. Bake the crisp for about 30 minutes or until the top is golden brown and the apples are tender and bubbling.
5. Serve the crisp warm or at room temperature, with ice cream if desired.

Oatmeal Cookies

CHUCK: *I don't know whether oatmeal or chocolate chip cookies are America's favorites, but these big treats are always a hit with anyone in need of a sweet snack that's still relatively good for you. Pour a glass of milk or cider and chomp on a few—perfection! Not surprisingly, Wyatt is usually poking around the kitchen when these are fresh from the oven.* Makes about 16 cookies

¾ cup light brown sugar

2 tablespoons soy butter or unsalted butter

1 large egg, lightly beaten

¼ cup unsweetened applesauce, preferably organic

2 tablespoons low-fat or nonfat milk

1 cup unbleached all-purpose flour

½ teaspoon ground cinnamon

¼ teaspoon baking soda

1¼ cups rolled oats

½ cup dried currants or raisins

1. Preheat the oven to 350°F. Lightly grease 2 baking sheets.
2. In the bowl of an electric mixer fitted with the paddle attachment, mix the sugar and butter on medium speed until blended, 2 to 3 minutes. Add the egg and beat for 1 minute longer.
3. With the mixer running, slowly add the applesauce and milk and beat for about 1 minute. Turn off the mixer and scrape the sides of the bowl.
4. In another bowl, whisk together the flour, cinnamon, and baking soda. Add the dry ingredients to the mixing bowl in 1 or 2 additions and blend on medium-low speed after each addition until smooth. This should take about 2 minutes.
5. Add the oats and currants or raisins and stir into the batter with the mixer on low speed. If it's easier, stir the oats and currants into the batter by hand.

6. Drop the cookies by teaspoonfuls onto the baking sheets, leaving about 2 inches between each one. Bake for 13 to 15 minutes or until the cookies are lightly browned and beginning to crisp around the edges.

7. Let the cookies cool on the baking sheets for 4 to 5 minutes and then transfer to wire racks to cool completely.

RACHEL'S TIP

Happier chickens produce healthier eggs. Chickens that range freely on grass lay eggs with half the cholesterol and more vitamin E, beta-carotene, and omega-3's than eggs from non-free range chickens.

Seasonal Chart for Fruits and Vegetables

With the food industry's ability to ship produce from one country to another, most of the fruits and vegetables listed here can be found in markets just about any time of year. While this is true, Sheryl and I try to eat in season as often as possible. For this chart, we selected fruits and vegetables that are best when eaten ripe from local suppliers and farmers.

Because our country is enormous, growing seasons differ from state to state. Therefore, we have been generous with our time spans. Clearly, strawberries ripen in Texas in early spring, while they may not appear in Vermont gardens until mid-June.

We have left out those vegetables that are always in the markets (i.e., onions, carrots, and lettuce). Those that are flagged with ** are abundantly available all year long and so many folks may consider them "seasonless." It is our experience that they are best when eaten in season.

FRUITS AND VEGETABLES IN SEASON

	JAN	FEB	MAR	APR	MAY	JUNE	JULY	AUG	SEPT	OCT	NOV	DEC
**APPLES	■	■	■	■	■				■	■	■	■
ARTICHOKES			■	■	■	■			■	■	■	■
ASPARAGUS		■	■	■	■	■						
**AVOCADOS	■	■	■									
**BEANS, GREEN				■	■	■	■	■				
**BEETS								■	■	■	■	
BLUEBERRIES					■	■	■	■				
**BROCCOLI	■	■	■		■				■	■	■	■
BRUSSELS SPROUTS		■	■	■	■				■	■	■	■

FRUITS AND VEGETABLES IN SEASON

	JAN	FEB	MAR	APR	MAY	JUNE	JULY	AUG	SEPT	OCT	NOV	DEC
**CABBAGE						●	●	●	●	●	●	
CANTALOUPE					●	●	●	●	●			
**CAULIFLOWER	●	●	●	●	●				●	●	●	●
CHERRIES, SWEET					●	●	●	●				
CORN						●	●	●	●	●		
CRANBERRIES									●	●	●	●
**CUCUMBER					●	●	●	●	●			
EGGPLANT							●	●	●	●		
FENNEL	●	●	●							●	●	●
**GRAPES					●	●	●	●	●	●	●	
LEEKS									●	●	●	●
ORANGES	●	●	●	●	●						●	●
PEACHES					●	●	●	●				
PEARS	●	●	●					●	●	●	●	●
PEAS				●	●	●	●	●	●	●		
PEPPERS, SWEET							●	●	●	●	●	●
PEPPERS, HOT							●	●	●	●	●	
PINEAPPLES				●	●	●	●					
PLUMS					●	●	●	●	●	●		
**POTATOES	●	●	●						●	●	●	
RASPBERRIES						●	●	●	●	●		
**SPINACH		●	●	●	●							
STRAWBERRIES					●	●	●					
SUMMER SQUASH						●	●	●	●			

(yellow, zucchini, patty pan, crookneck)

	JAN	FEB	MAR	APR	MAY	JUNE	JULY	AUG	SEPT	OCT	NOV	DEC
SWEET POTATOES								●	●	●	●	●
TOMATO						●	●	●	●	●		
WATERMELON					●	●	●	●	●			
WINTER SQUASH										●	●	●

(butternut, acorn, Hubbard, delicata, pumpkin, spaghetti, kabocha, turban)

Acknowledgments

Thank you to Kathy Huck, who spearheaded this challenging project, and to St. Martin's Press for their tremendous support in allowing me to share Chef Chuck with the world and hopefully providing an easy and delicious route to those who are looking to integrate health with cooking.

Special thanks to Rebecca Oliver, for believing in the concept from the beginning and for working so hard to make sure it became a reality.

Victoria Pearson, whose ability to capture the essence of these special meals with images so stunningly beautiful that I could almost eat the pages—I am amazed at your vision and artistic gifts.

Mary Goodbody, who was beautifully sensitive to my message and gave voice to my random thoughts.

Special thanks to Pam Wertheimer, without whose tenacity and talent at managing my life and a billion other fires simultaneously, no one would be seeing this book for another year.

To my sister, Kathy Crow, who took on the tremendous weight of managing my part of this time-consuming project. You made it easy and fun. Thank you, thank you, thank you.

To my parents, who set the bar in so many ways and taught us that meals together feed not only our bodies, but also our souls. This is a gift that will surely be passed on to my children, and hopefully their children.

To Corrie White, thank you for being such a huge and delightful part of this project, in my kitchen, and on the road. I feel blessed to call you and Chuck friends.

To Rachel Beller for her love of knowledge, where nutrition and wellness intersect. You have forever changed the way I look at what I put into my body.

And to Chuck White, whose sensitivity to my health history and my consequent desire for healthfulness of every meal served at home or on the road is the special ingredient of every recipe within these pages. Your culinary knowledge and creativity have enhanced my life. I am grateful for the opportunity you have given me to shine a bright light on your beautiful gift . . . the gift of healthy cooking.

—SHERYL

I would like to thank my amazing wife, Corrie, for being the most wonderful person I know and for making me a better man.

To my family, I'm lucky to have such a supportive "cast." I'm glad they still keep me around. And, although she never thought I'd be a chef, I have to especially thank my mother, Martie, for all the inspiring dishes I grew up eating, and the ones I still enjoy today.

There are several chefs in my career who have greatly influenced me. Many thanks to Paul Wade, Willie Thomas, Patrice Piralla, and Giovanni Giosa.

To Pam Wertheimer and Scooter Weintraub, Sheryl's management, who have taken great care of me over the last several years. To Kathy Crow, for her creative input, wittiness, and diligent time spent helping Sheryl with this book.

This book would be nothing without the brilliance of Mary Goodbody, who helped pull the ideas out of my head and translate them onto paper. She helped mold the giant ball of clay into a very nice piece of work.

To Rachel Beller and her expertise in helping educate Sheryl and me on healthy ways of eating and living.

Thanks to William Morris Endeavor, especially Rebecca Oliver, for looking out for our best interests and guiding us throughout this process.

To Kathy Huck, who rocks, and *all* the wonderful people at St. Martin's Press.

Much appreciation to Victoria Pearson and the talented people surrounding her, including Pam Morris and Valerie Aikman-Smith. Vicki is a genius at what she does and is so much fun to be around.

And finally, quite possibly the greatest thank-you goes to Sheryl for approaching me with the idea for this book. Despite my uncertainty, she assured me that "we're going to do this." And now, we have. I don't have words to describe how incredible she is, and how truly blessed I am to be able to cook for her and her family.

—CHUCK

Index